KU-739-417

Heinz and Geneste Kurth
BARBECUE
and the joy of cooking on an open fire

Please note that metric measures in this book are not exact conversions but have been rounded up.

Other titles in the series
By Heinz and Geneste Kurth
OUTDOOR HOLIDAYS for indoor people

Text and Illustrations © Heinz and Geneste Kurth 1979

First published in Great Britain in 1979

This paperback edition published and distributed in Great Britain in 1983 by the Automobile Association, Fanum House, Basingstoke, Hampshire RG21 2EA

Casebound edition published by B. T. Batsford Ltd.

Created and Produced by Ventura Publishing Ltd., 44 Uxbridge Street, London W8 7TG

All Rights Reserved. No part of this publication may be reproduced, stored in a retrieval system, or transmitted, in any form or by any means, electronic, mechanical, photocopying, recording, or otherwise, without the prior permission of the Publishers

ISBN 0 86145 172 4   AA Ref. 65977

Printed in Spain by Editorial Fher SA, Bilbao

contents

Fire, food and civilisation

Fire, the gift of the gods, was tamed by our ancestors to keep them warm and to make raw meat taste better – in fact they often roasted whole animals on spits made of hardwood.

An open fire may also have grilled the sausages and fowl shown in the Bayeux tapestry. William the Conqueror is seen here taking part in a sumptuous meal, sitting on the right of Odo, the Bishop of Bayeux. It is a royal occasion but there are no spoons on the table and forks had not yet been invented. Eating was a manly and casual affair – guests brought their own knives with which to cut the meat.

Later, in Chaucer's time, roasting spits and forks were made of wrought iron, and charcoal fires cooked and browned delicious meats under the professional eye of a kitchen master. Banquets lasted for many hours and sometimes more than a hundred different fish, meat, game, sweet and cheese dishes appeared on the table together with tankards of mead and goblets of wine. There was no television then to interrupt these joyful occasions, though live entertainment formed part of any good banquet: jugglers and mummers performed their tricks between the tables and minstrels played romantic airs until well into the night by the light of candles and torches.

Fire has also played its part in forging the steel for modern cooking ranges. But the heat produced by today's gleaming kitchen equipment lacks the aroma that is imparted by a wood fire or the mellow glow of burning charcoal.

Barbecuing brings out the flavours which our ancestors enjoyed while solving another modern problem: how to experience something different without spending a lot of money in the process. Galloping inflation has affected people in many countries and altered their way of life. One of the effects of this has been that dining-out regularly is now beyond most people's pocket.

Barbecuing offers a genuine solution to this difficulty because it enables a meal to be produced at home using the choicest cuts of meat and a memorable wine at a third of the price that would be charged in a first class restaurant.

Taming an open barbecue fire can be a delightful and romantic break from normal household routine especially when friends and relations join in to provide an 'evening-out' by themselves and for themselves.

How fire roasts, grills and smokes

When charcoal burns, oxygen from the air combines with it to produce heat, smoke and carbon monoxide gas. Since hot air always rises, the gas and smoke are carried upwards until they mix with cooler air and disperse. For this process to continue, a fresh supply of air needs to be allowed in from below, and this is done by building the fire on a grate in which are slots small enough to let the air through without allowing the charcoal pieces to drop down.

A space underneath the grate makes fire-lighting easy; a few crumpled sheets of newspaper and some twigs can be pushed in and lit with a match, and this will ignite the charcoal very quickly.

In the absence of a firegrate, charcoal placed in a tray that has no holes will not ignite or burn easily since air cannot reach the pieces in the centre. This can be overcome however if the tray is first lined with heavy duty aluminium foil and covered with a layer of pebbles. The foil lining reflects the heat and makes cleaning easier and if it is tucked well over the rim of the tray so that it stays in place it should last a season. The pebbles should be spread out to make a bed about $1\frac{1}{2}$ in (4 cm) deep and this allows air from above to reach all the charcoal pieces through the narrow gaps between the pebbles. To prevent grease and ashes clogging the fire base, the pebbles should be cleaned in a bucket of hot water and detergent after every five or six barbecues.

Burning charcoal (1) emits strong infra-red radiation. Your hand may feel only moderately hot just over the grill but the heat is really quite powerful and cooking times are often shorter than anticipated.

Each metal bar of the grill (2) absorbs and conducts a large amount of heat, and this is what produces the typical burn-marks on barbecued meat.

Fat from the meat drips onto the charcoal (3), burns and causes flare-ups. Remedies: trim off excess fat; douse locally with water from a small garden spray; or place a drip-pan made of aluminium foil under the meat and bank the charcoal up on either side.

Anything that gets in the way will cut off the infra-red radiation, and this includes the film of ash (4) which always forms on the burning charcoal. Knock the ash off for maximum heat but leave it on for slow cooking.

FUEL FOR THE FIRE

Charcoal is a remarkable fuel. Blacksmiths' bellows can raise its temperature to around 1500°C to melt iron and a small heap of about twenty pieces will burn for over an hour. Charcoal is bought in the form of pressed briquets or as lumpwood charcoal. Briquets have a fairly uniform heat output, burn a little longer but lack the typical charcoal smell. Kiln-charred lumpwood charcoal comes in uneven pieces, ignites easily but gives off sparks.

Whichever type you buy, look for a good quality product and continue buying the same brand so that your fire radiates a consistent heat. Buy large rather than small bags (per fire they work out much cheaper) and store them in a dry place.

Wood is commonly used for smoke-curing and smoke-cooking and is dealt with on page 56.

Bottled or piped gas is convenient and reliable to use but needs expensive fittings. In some barbecue models, the burning gas heats up special pieces of rock and the cooking is done on the heat transmitted by the rock.

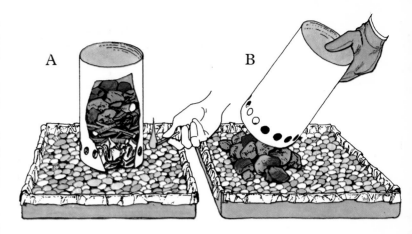

LIGHTING THE FIRE

If the fire is in a tray that has no holes, one of the quickest methods is to light the charcoal in a 'chimney'. The bottom is cut out of a tall tin and air-holes punched into the lower rim. The tin is placed on the firebed and filled up as shown. Then, when the charcoal is alight, the tin is removed (using a thick glove as it will be very hot) and the glowing charcoal spreads out over the firebed. The glowing pieces can be raked out to form an even layer (see drawing above).

Another method is to use liquid fire starters such as methylated or white spirit which are poured over a small mound of charcoal in the firetray. It takes a minute or two for the liquid to soak in and during this time the cap of the spirit container should be replaced carefully. The charcoal should then be lit with a long match or taper. *Caution:* it is not only dangerous to use petrol or paraffin to start the fire, but these highly inflammable liquids also impart an unpleasant taste to the food.

Solid fire lighters can be bought in the form of blocks or granules. In the case of blocks they should be broken up into smaller pieces and inserted under a mound of charcoal before being lit.

Whichever method is used to light the fire, cooking should commence only after the charcoal begins to show a surface of grey or white ash.

Improvised and simple barbecues

Very few materials are needed to build a simple barbecue on which to cook a meal and gain experience. Some improvisations are shown below and a few large stones or just the ground itself with a hole dug into it can serve. The only critical dimension is the distance from the top of the charcoal to the grill which should be adjustable from about 2 in (5 cm) for fast searing to about 5 in (12 cm) for slow cooking. Two bricks can serve as supports for the grill, their shape allowing the grilling surface to be placed at different levels by simply turning the bricks over while the grill is supported for a moment by a long stick.

All manner of improvised bases can and have been used, like drainpipes, plinths of bricks, low walls and wheelbarrows. Naturally any base should be firm and must not topple, particularly if bumped against by a child.

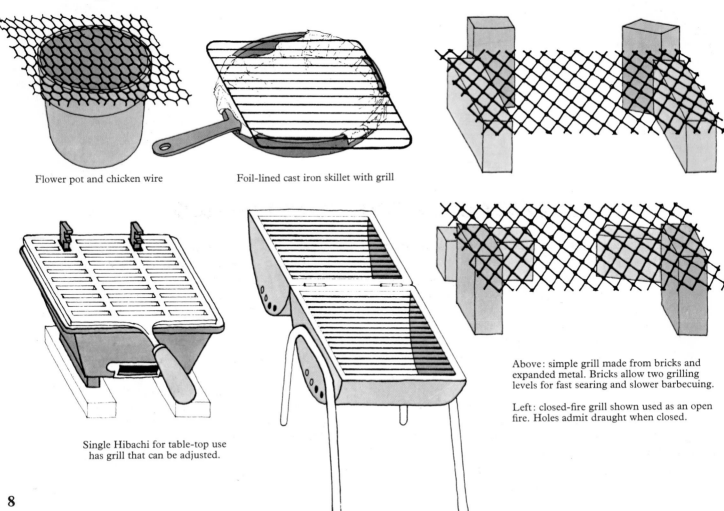

Flower pot and chicken wire

Foil-lined cast iron skillet with grill

Single Hibachi for table-top use has grill that can be adjusted.

Above: simple grill made from bricks and expanded metal. Bricks allow two grilling levels for fast searing and slower barbecuing.

Left: closed-fire grill shown used as an open fire. Holes admit draught when closed.

Wheel barrow filled with earth and topped with pebbles

A trial barbecue to serve two

Choose a steak about 1 in (2.5 cm) thick weighing not less than $1\frac{1}{2}$ lb ($\frac{3}{4}$ kg). Look for one that is well marbled with thin streaks of fat. Sprinkle some pepper over both sides but not salt which draws out the juices, so it is added after cooking.

It is important to serve barbecued meat as soon as it is cooked, as uncovered food soon goes cold out of doors. So prepare your salad, open the wine in advance and have hot plates ready by the time the meat is cooked.

Brush the grill with vegetable oil or put a fork through a folded piece of streaky bacon or fat trimmings and rub it over the grill to prevent the meat from sticking.

As soon as the charcoal has turned grey, after about 20 minutes, put on your mittens and use long tongs to place the meat on the grill which should be about 2 in (5 cm) above the charcoal. After a minute, raise the grill to about 5 in (12 cm) for slower cooking and give it another six minutes for medium done or eight minutes for well done. Then turn it over, lower the grill again and repeat.

But do not rely on these cooking times since wind, fuel amounts and draught conditions vary.

It is safer, after a total cooking time of about twelve minutes, to make a cut in the middle or the thickest part of the meat to check its colour.

Open fire brazier. Grill is raised by turning it round a screw.

Open fire, shielded by a hood. The spit is hand-rotated.

In this hooded barbecue, a movable firebox can be placed horizontally for grilling and vertically for spit-roasting.

Closed-fire wagon grill has rotisserie driven from electricity mains. Equipped with temperature gauge, warming oven and glass doors.

Gas-fired kettle grill with vents. has two fixed grill heights.

Types of barbecue

Barbecues are designed to cook food either by direct heat in open-fire models or by reflected heat in closed-fire models.

OPEN FIRE BARBECUES

Open fire barbecues are ideal for fast-grilling steaks, pieces of chicken, chops, sausages and hamburgers. But a means of adjusting the height of the grill to vary the heat is essential: a low position is needed to sear the meat and seal in the juices, and a high position for longer cooking without burning.

Hibachis (literally meaning 'fire-ball') from Japan have a cast iron body with draught controls which are opened to start the fire and partly closed to slow it down. When buying a brazier it is advisable to look for a model with an adjustable grill. Hibachis and braziers are also made with either fixed or folding legs; working at waist height makes cooking safer and less back-aching.

Flat, low-level picnic barbecues are very enjoyable on sunny days. Folded up, they can be stowed comfortably in the boot of a car.

WINDSHIELDS

A windshield will protect the hot area of the grill from wind and will stop sparks and smoke becoming a nuisance in sudden gusts. On some barbecue models, the windshield also forms the support for a roasting spit. They are also useful in that they form a ready support for closed-fire cooking.

CLOSED FIRE BARBECUES

These have a lid or hood which reflects heat downwards and contains it, thus browning the meat from the top and sides. They are also used for roasts and for whole chicken on spits which require longer cooking times. Since prolonged cooking produces much dripping fat, the charcoal fire is usually banked to the side rather than directly under the meat, making room for a drip-pan to catch the fat.

With the lid completely closed, temperatures are raised or lowered by means of vents which control the draught and alter the rate at which the charcoal burns. When the cooking is finished, vents in the lid can be closed to snuff out the fire, so saving unburnt charcoal. An open-fire grill can easily be converted into a closed one by making a wire hood covered with aluminium foil as shown.

SMOKE-COOKING

Smoke-cooking is done on a closed fire barbecue. While the heat from the charcoal cooks the food, damp wood chips, sawdust, herbs or leaves are added to the fire to impart their aroma to the food. Smoke-cooking produces some of the most memorable meals in that the aroma builds a kind of bridge between the food itself and the wine that is drunk with it.

SMOKE-CURING

This method requires less heat but the smoky wood fire may have to be kept going for many hours in a special smoke oven as described on page 59. Commercial smoke-curing is becoming a rarity because refrigeration is a better preservation method although it does not improve the taste. Freshly smoked eel, herring, ribs and chicken are very tasty delicacies that can be served either as a first course or as the main dish.

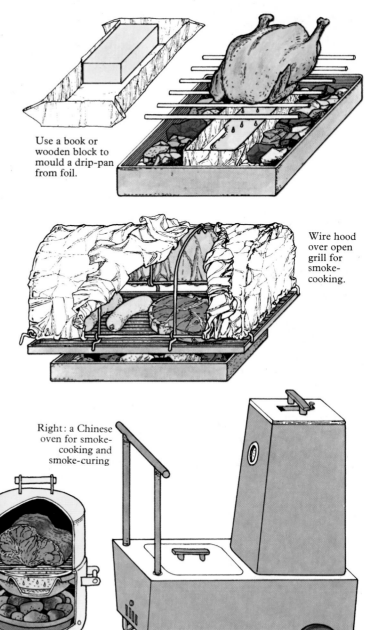

Use a book or wooden block to mould a drip-pan from foil.

Wire hood over open grill for smoke-cooking.

Right: a Chinese oven for smoke-cooking and smoke-curing

Right: this versatile kettle-cooker can be used in a variety of ways. As a barbecue grill as shown at A; as a smoke oven when a built-in pan is filled with a marinade to baste the meat by condensation; as a roaster or as a steam cooker as shown at B, when the pan is filled with water to keep fish or meat moist during cooking.

A

B

Choosing a barbecue

Experimenting with an improvised layout will have given you an idea of what barbecuing is about and you may now want a more convenient model or a permanent structure. The type you buy or build depends on what you want to spend, on where you live, how often you want to cook and what type of cooking you want to do.

PERMANENT INDOOR BARBECUES

The advantage of an indoor barbecue is that it allows cooking whatever the weather or time of day. Indoor barbecues are permanent installations that can be built as part of a kitchen range or into an existing fireplace, and they must be erected on sound and fireproof foundations. This means that wherever oven-hot bricks or stones are in contact with an existing structure they need to be insulated and, most importantly, require a canopy or hood that will gather all the smoke and dangerous carbon monoxide gas and carry them outside via a flue or chimney. An efficient extractor fan may be needed in order to lead the fumes round awkward corners, and this sort of installation is specialist work.

Whether you build inside or out – but particularly inside – it is advisable to show a plan of the barbecue to your local building inspector to make sure that your barbecue is not only safe in use but also does not become a nuisance to your neighbours.

Below: a counter unit with sink, grill and working space all at the same level is probably the ideal indoor combination. Note fire-door and large canopy.
Right: free standing barbecue has square-shaped hood to echo the angular look of the barbecue.

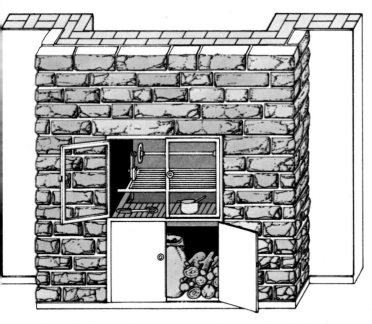

OUTDOOR BARBECUES

To many people only the sunny outdoors offers the right setting for barbecue cooking, and eating straight from the grill with an occasional whiff of fragrant herbs in the air is indeed one of the delightful pleasures which life can offer.

Of course, it all depends on the climate in which you live, but even winter weather need not stop the barbecue from doing its delicious work. The main part of the meal, the meat for instance, can be cooked outside and when ready, be brought into the house where bread, salad and wine are already served and oven-heated plates keep the meat hot until it is eaten.

Nor does sudden rain need to spoil a dinner. Only two things have to stay dry: the cook himself and the grill. A raincoat with hood will keep the cook dry but umbrellas or sunshades held over the barbecue are soon perforated by sparks and set alight. Closed fires go on cooking merrily in a downpour and a metal lid placed over a shielded fire will keep the rain away. It is only the flat-topped open fire from which food may have to be transferred to the kitchen.

Above: barbecue built into a fireplace. Glass doors seal-in the smoke and keep the heat near the meat. Storage locker underneath. Below: a simple fireplace conversion. Note hood and hotplate for coffee etc.

PORTABLE OR PERMANENT

A portable barbecue can be turned to an angle at which it is least affected by wind and if it rains it can be wheeled under a shelter. Another consideration when choosing a barbecue is how often it will be in use. Barbecuing should be a casual enjoyment and wheeling a portable model out from its storage place and returning it after use may be too much bother.

A permanent structure on the other hand is ready for cooking at any time and a well designed barbecue can be an attractive feature even when it is not in use. A roofed patio or a recessed porch are ideal locations for it and an extra wall or a tall hedge can sometimes be introduced to give shelter in exposed places, the warm glow from the fire soon becoming a culinary focus for friends and family alike.

Many people treat barbecuing as a special occasion and ration its use to perhaps one meal a week. For that amount of cooking, the barbecue can be very simple in design since complicated arrangements needed for spit-roasting and plate warming cupboards merely duplicate kitchen facilities and duplication means extra worry and extra maintanance.

Whether you decide on a portable or permanent model, make sure that there is enough level ground near the barbecue for cooking, serving and dining – flagstones or concrete are a better surface than grass which wears out and becomes slippery after rain. And if there is an unobstructed path to the kitchen door, plates, bowls and used dishes can be carried so much more easily.

COOKING FOR EIGHT OR EIGHTY

Small barbecues produce a surprisingly large amount of food. The hibachi shown on page 10 cooks steaks or chicken pieces for up to four diners at one go and when catering regularly for more, another hibachi can be added.

Basically, a grill of about 12×20 in (30×50 cm) is adequate for a party of up to eight but it is always a good idea to choose a larger grill than is actually needed since it is possible to build a small fire under a large grill but not the other way round.

A practical way to cater for very large parties is to prepare as much as possible in the conventional kitchen and then do only the essential cooking on the barbecue, serving each tray load in shifts; women and children first and red-haired sailors last or whichever grouping best helps strangers to become acquainted.

Something else to bear in mind is how many types of cooking you want to do. This book describes mainly open fire methods which have a relatively short cooking time, while spit roasting for instance may take many hours and requires more elaborate equipment.

Building a simple, open fire barbecue

The best time to build a barbecue is when other outside building work is being done or when the layout of a garden area is being changed. It is then that barbecue, walls, shelter and surfacing can be planned and built as a whole. And if you like to work with bricks and mortar, you can do the whole or part of the job yourself. Alternatively, if you decide to employ a builder for the job, the following pages will be useful for issuing your instructions.

The barbecue illustrated here is a simple, waist-high basic unit to which extra elements such as storage cupboards and worktops can be added to suit your particular location. A working surface next to and on a level with the grill is essential for preparing the food, checking that it is cooked, and transferring it to plates, as well as for putting down accessories until they are needed.

METAL PARTS

The size of the firegrate and grill governs the overall dimensions of the barbecue so these parts need to be found or bought first. Grills can be made of cast iron, of expanded metal set into a frame, or of $\frac{3}{16}$ in (4 mm) steel rods welded to a steel frame.

Shelves from old cookers or refrigerators make excellent grills and those made of stainless steel will last a very long time. Two shelves can be placed side by side to make a larger grill and it is useful to buy a spare set at the same time for replacing a grill that has burnt through.

There are two ways of varying the intensity of the heat; either by moving the grill or by moving the firebase. In the barbecue illustrated, the grill is moved manually from one set of iron brackets to the next. As the grill is very hot, oven gloves to protect the hands or two rods about two feet (60 cm) long are necessary for lifting and sliding the grill from one position to another.

The iron or mild steel brackets should be at least $\frac{3}{16}$ in (4 mm) thick and you will need eight of them for the two grill positions.

The elevating grill makes the construction of a firebase very easy. The charcoal can lie on either a framed grate or in a tray lined with foil and pebbles or simply on a floor made of firebrick and lined with foil. Neither the grill nor the firebase should be cemented into place but should remain free to expand with the heat from the fire and contract with frost in winter.

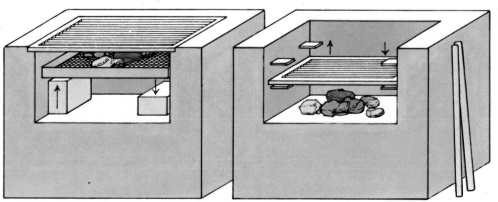

Using bricks as support for firebase.

Changing grill-level manually from one bracket to another.

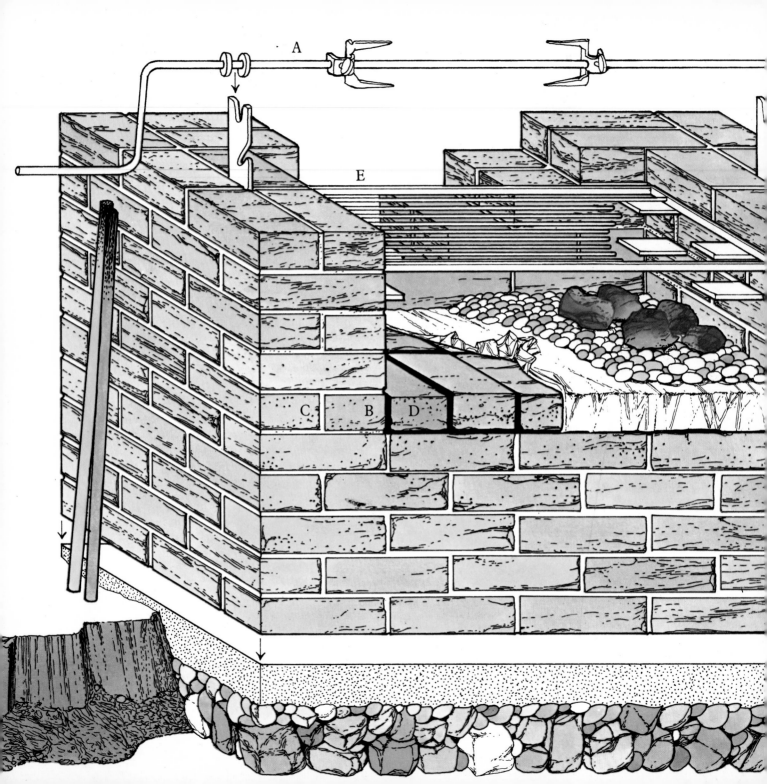

I

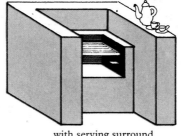

basic unit

with serving surround

working top over storage cupboards and windshield

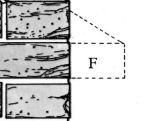

C

F

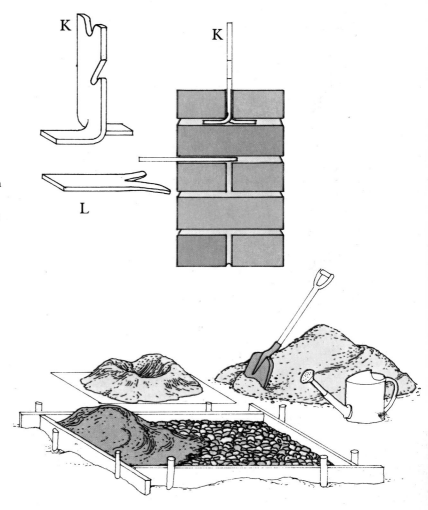

K

K

L

A Simple, hand-wound roasting spit rests on 2 slotted supports. Spit can be rotated at two levels depending on dimensions of roast and degree of heat required. Roasts on the spit have to be balanced so that they turn easily – so attach counterweights to roast or spit.

B Firebricks (shown purple)

C Ordinary bricks

D Loose bricks (covered in foil)

E Grill, resting on brackets

F Position for brick-ledge, supporting working top

G Concrete foundation 3 in (8 cm) deep

H Hardcore under, 6 in (15 cm) deep

I Alternative layouts, using the same barbecue unit.

K Typical iron support for spit

L Swallow-tailed bracket for grill

G

H

HOTPLATE

This is not an essential but sometimes a useful addition to barbecue cooking. Made of cast iron or aluminium, the hot plate replaces part of the grill and serves as a surface on which to cook greasy meats or pancakes, or to toast bread and rolls and keep coffee and soups hot. A hotplate that has a lip or runnel round the edges will prevent fat from dripping down into the fire. It should however cover only part of the grilling area; if it covered it completely, the fire would be snuffed out unless updraught could escape through a chimney as shown on page 19.

CONCRETE FOUNDATION

Once the size of the grill has been established the next step is to lay out the first brick course loosely and outline the area needed for the foundation. Where the earth is firm, concrete may be poured directly into a pit of the same dimensions as the concrete slab is to be. When digging the earth out, make sure that the base and the sides are level.

In crumbly soil, the excavation should be somewhat larger to make room for a retaining frame of oiled wood to contain the concrete. When the concrete has set, the frame is removed. The frame also provides an accurate guide when levelling the surface of the concrete slab.

When the pit has been half filled, lay reinforcing steel rods or wire mesh into it. Continue filling, taking care to tamp the new concrete through the mesh so that it binds with the earlier layer.

Concrete mix: 1 part cement, 3 parts sand, 4 parts coarse aggregate (shingle or gravel).

BRICKWORK

Most barbecues are built of brick which is easy to handle and gives a neat appearance. While most of the structure can be made of common bricks, those lining the fire area should be either firebricks (made for the purpose, but expensive) or 'overburnt' bricks which can be bought for a little extra at most builders' yards.

These bricks stand up to the heat from the charcoal and do not crack like ordinary house or 'green' bricks. It is as well to remember that bricks should be damp but not wet when they are laid; that a spirit level helps to make sure that the courses are level, and that mortar joints look neater if they are smoothed with the point of a trowel. After two days, when the mortar has dried, give the brickwork a rub-down with a wad of sacking and fine sand – this will take off any unsightly mortar splashes.

Mortar mix for bricks: 1 part cement, 4½ parts clean fine sand and ½ part fireclay (or lime) to add elasticity.

STONE

Natural stone and concrete blocks are very decorative outdoor building materials. When barbecues are built with them the area around the fire is commonly lined with firebricks (end on) while the stones or blocks are continued on the outside as a veneer. Granite or basalt do not need this lining since their volcanic origin makes them proof against high temperatures – unlike shale, sandstone or limestone.

Mortar for stone has to be richer than that for bricks: 1 part cement, 3 parts fine sand and ½ part fireclay (or lime).

Before you reach the top course of bricks, do not forget a shelf to support the work-top. Two or three bricks laid at right angles so that they protrude will easily hold up one side of a concrete or marble slab. The other side can be supported either by brick columns or by a small brick wall as shown on page 14. For casting a suitable concrete slab, use the same method as when casting a lintel (see page 21).

When the brick or stone work is complete and the mortar has set, fill the interior with earth or gravel almost up to the firebase and top it with a platform of bricks laid loose onto the earth. Use firebricks if they are to be your actual firebase.

Building a combined barbecue and smoke-oven

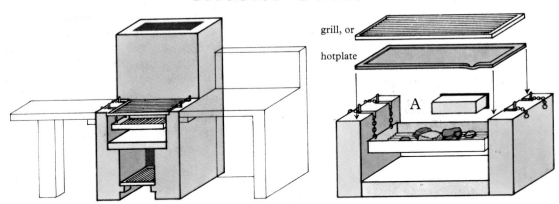

grill, or

hotplate

A

This is the Savoy-touch in barbecuing, bringing together the facilities for several different cooking methods – grilling, roasting, smoke-cooking and smoke-curing. Have you ever tried a leg of tender, aromatic, oakwood-smoked chicken? Only one snag: your friends will come to live with you and never go away!

Again, only the basic unit is shown while worktops and other features can be added as required.

THE BARBECUE UNIT

This may be equipped with a simple elevating grill as shown on page 16 or alternatively with an elevating grate as illustrated here. Beneath the permanent (but not cemented-in) grill, a fire-grate is raised or lowered by means of a chain. The chain can be handled with bare hands since the transmission of heat from link to link is negligible. Winding gallows can be bought ready made, but shown here is a simpler version for home construction in which the chains are adjusted by hand and secured on upright metal spikes.

Metal parts needed for the barbecue unit are a grill, a framed fire-grate with four chains attached and four metal spikes.

Since the barbecue has a chimney, a hinged hotplate covering the whole grill area can also be installed. Before it is used however, brick A at the back of the fire area has to be loose so that it can be taken out to open up an air passage to the chimney. When barbecuing is resumed, the brick must be replaced.

THE SMOKE OVEN

This part of the barbecue has a separate fire chamber with a wide opening into the rectangular chimney where the food is hung for smoke-cooking or -curing. A factory chimney would be round and tapering so as to generate a strong updraught and a roaring fire, but the principle of a smoke oven is quite different: the wide chimney not only allows plenty of space for the food but it helps to slow down the passage of heat and smoke. A cover in front of the fire area creates a poor draught so that the wood fire is almost starved of air and burns slowly, encouraging heat and smoke to stay in the chimney as long as possible, warming the masonry and curing the food before they are finally allowed to escape through tiny vent holes in the chimney cover.

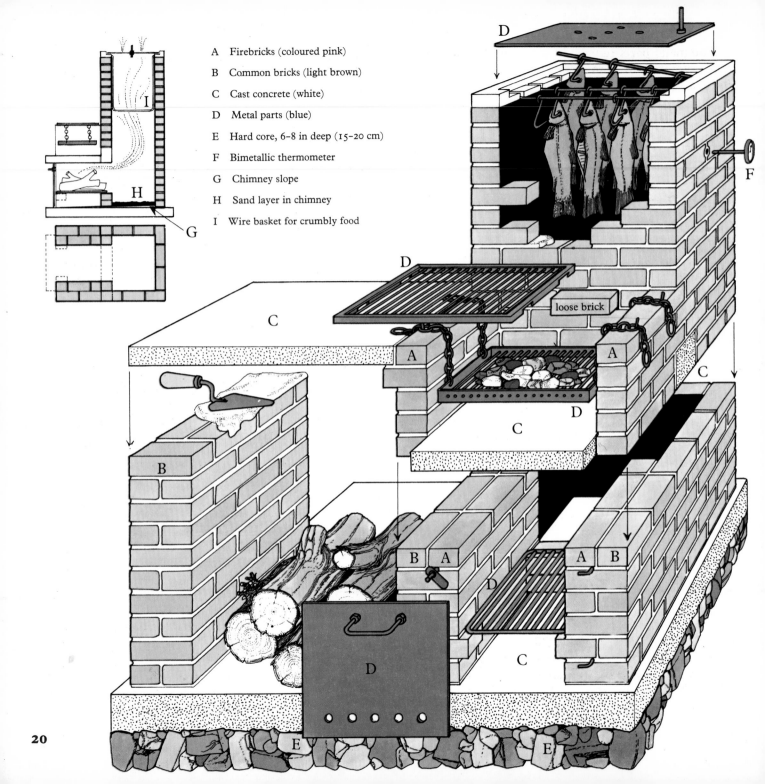

A   Firebricks (coloured pink)

B   Common bricks (light brown)

C   Cast concrete (white)

D   Metal parts (blue)

E   Hard core, 6-8 in deep (15-20 cm)

F   Bimetallic thermometer

G   Chimney slope

H   Sand layer in chimney

I   Wire basket for crumbly food

loose brick

The metal parts required for the smoke oven are a fire-grate of about $\frac{1}{4}$ in (5 mm) cast iron or ordinary steel, a rectangular chimney cover of $\frac{1}{16}$ in (2 mm) sheet metal with vent holes, a panel of the same thickness with vent holes to cover the front opening of the fire chamber, a number of steel rods plus wire hooks from which to suspend the food, and eighteen $\frac{1}{4}$ in (5 mm) steel rods and a sheet of expanded metal for reinforcing the concrete. You will also need a thermometer – ideally one that has a dial for outside reading.

FOUNDATION

Prepare the ground and cast the concrete base in the same way as described on page 18 but build a deeper bed of rubble underneath, about 6 in (15 cm) – and cast the concrete foundation at least 4 in (10 cm) thick.

BRICKWORK

Lay the first brick course as accurately as you can, squaring up the corners and making the mortar joints about $\frac{1}{2}$ in (1.5 cm) thick. Use a chisel to split off a third of each of two bricks, set them across so that they jut out and form a ledge as shown; they will later support the fire grate in front, while the back will be supported by another two bricks laid loose on the ground. These bricks can be removed from time to time to allow easy access when cleaning out the chimney base. Stop the brickwork when you have completed the sixth course, on which the lintel and the fire-cover are to rest.

This is also a good time to build up a slope towards the back of the chimney floor either with concrete or with left-over mortar. This will allow any rainwater that enters the chimney to flow out towards the front of the fire area.

LINTEL AND FIRE-COVER

The lintel should be two bricks deep and a header wide in order to have the strength to support the bricks above it. But the non load-bearing fire-cover

need only be one brick deep. Cast both units early on so that they can set and cure before being placed in the structure.

MOULDS

So that the lintel and fire-cover will fit neatly into the brickwork, much trouble can be saved by casting them to the same module as the bricks, using actual bricks to make temporary moulds as shown and not forgetting to allow for the $\frac{1}{2}$ in (1 cm) mortar joints. Lay the bricks for the mould on a sheet of plastic and paint both bricks and base with mould oil (engine oil will serve instead) then line the base and the sides of the mould with sheets of plastic. Make the corners watertight with adhesive tape to prevent any loss of grout, and paint mould oil generously between any sheets that overlap.

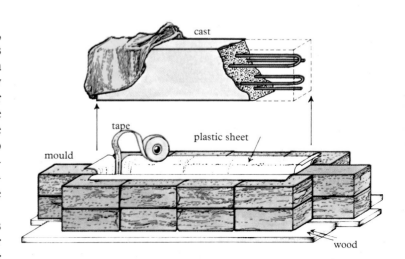

CASTING

Since it is prudent to allow at least four days for the cast to set properly, this work is best done when the nights are free of frost – frost interrupts and even prevents the setting and curing processes. Use fresh cement which makes a tough concrete and use as little water as possible – just enough to make the mix workable.

Mix for lintel and cover: 1 part cement, 2 parts sand and 3 parts coarse aggregate – ideally crushed firebrick pieces of ⅛ to ¾ in (3-20 mm).

Mix the dry ingredients thoroughly, then carefully add small measures of water. When it is ready, pack the mix gently into the mould, spreading and tamping it persistently until it forms a layer about 2 in (5 cm) thick and fills the corners tightly.

Lay the first three or four ¼ in (5 mm) steel rods on the surface of the concrete and cover them with another 2 in (5 cm) of concrete. Beat the mix lightly and rhythmically with a piece of wood so that the layers merge and air bubbles rise. Then place the remaining reinforcing in position and fill up the mould to the top. Cover the cast with a sheet of plastic to guard against rain or unwelcome drying out in hot weather. When the concrete has set (after about 24 hours) replace the covering with damp sacking and keep it moist until the cast is ready to be moved.

Make a mould for the fire-cover and cast it in the same way as the lintel, using at least ten ¼ in (5 mm) steel rods, plus a sheet of expanded metal, for your reinforcement.

After four days, lintel and fire-cover can be taken out of their moulds and cemented in position but give the lintel another three days to cure before placing any bricks on it.

THE FINAL STAGE

Complete the brickwork as shown and do not forget to brick-in the bases of the four metal spikes for the barbecue chains and any protruding bricks you may need for supporting a working top. Allow also for thermometer holes: insert a thin wooden stick with a few layers of newspaper rolled around it in the fresh mortar – when the mortar has set, the stick can easily be removed. Use mortar to obtain a level rendering for the chimney top so that the metal cover will close it without any air gaps. But remember to make indentations in the mortar for the smoking rods from which the food is to be suspended.

Finally, cover the sloping chimney floor with ½ in (1 cm) of sand which will absorb any fat dripping down from the food. After a fortnight (which will seem very long!) when the smoke-oven has dried out and the concrete has cured, place the metal grate and the covers in position and light your first fire – make it a small one at first, lasting perhaps four hours which is enough to smoke-cure a bowlful of sprats. For recipes see pages 58–62.

MAINTENANCE

Outdoor barbecues have to stand up to fierce heat when in use as well as extreme cold in winter. A few simple rules will help to give your installation a longer life.

1. Do not heat up a newly built barbecue right away but allow two weeks for the cement to cure thoroughly. Then start gently with small fires first.

2. Cover the area of the grill to protect it from rain and winter weather – waterlogged brickwork may crack in a freeze-up or from the sudden heat of the fire.

3. Never douse charcoal on the firegrate but shovel it into a metal bucket filled with water from where it can later be taken out, dried and re-used.

4. After barbecuing, leave the grease from the cooking on the metal parts; it helps to prevent rusting. When you cook next, burn off the grease first and wipe the grill clean with a wad of newspaper. But always clean off ashes from the metal after using the barbecue since ash and moisture form lye, a nasty combination that attacks metal surfaces fast.

5. If you decide not to use the barbecue during the winter, you may want to protect removable metal parts by putting them into dry storage, at the same time painting a thin film of oil on all the other metal fixtures.

6. It is better not to place heavy pots or pans on a hot grill. Metal becomes weak when heated and a heavy weight will distort the grill's shape.

Cooking accessories

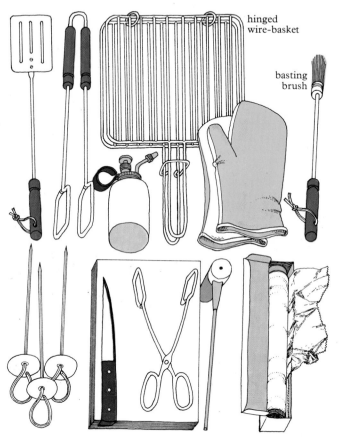

hinged wire-basket

basting brush

There is a large number of stylish gadgets on the market for anyone who wants to impress his guests but it is perhaps best to start with only a few and then add more when a real need emerges. If most of the initial preparation is done in the kitchen, outdoor utensils can be kept to a minimum so that all the chef's attention is focussed on the task of barbecuing his food to perfection.

First essentials for the chef are: thick oven gloves or mittens for handling the grill, hot foil and escaped pieces of charcoal: and a butcher's apron to protect clothing from burns and flying sparks. The apron pocket can hold a cloth on which to wipe his hands.

For cooking: long metal tongs with wooden or insulated handles, a sharp knife, cutting board and a pepper pot.

Later, as more dishes are tried: a hinged wire basket which is useful for holding crumbly food like fish and hamburgers over the fire; a long-handled basting brush (bristle, not nylon); some skewers with hand-shields for kebabs; a small garden spray filled with water to douse unwanted flames plus a wire brush to clean the grate.

ALUMINIUM FOIL

This versatile material might have been specially invented for barbecue chefs since its uses are endless both in cooking and serving. A large variety of disposable foil plates, cups and other containers is on the market. So are miles of rolled foil of varying widths and thicknesses.

The most useful foil in barbecuing is 'heavy-duty'; it is ideal for shaping drip-pans and wire hoods and for cooking sealed-in meat, fish, poultry and baked potatoes. If heavy-duty foil is not available, thinner foil can be used instead but the food must be double-wrapped. Some foil parcelled foods are laid directly onto the charcoal to cook separately while the meat is being grilled.

SERVING

A safe and pleasant way to serve a barbecued meal is on a firm table, using normal crockery and cutlery, including extra sharp knives for the meat. But large gatherings and children's parties can be fatal where treasured possessions are concerned; this is where plastic or disposable tableware comes into its own. Patterned paper napkins and decorative plastic or paper plates make an attractive, alfresco table setting.

Electric lights and candle glow

Even under a full moon barbecues need adequate lighting by which to see the food and also to prevent accidents. Probably the easiest to use are electric lamps fed from the mains via an underground cable, though these have to be installed by a qualified electrician.

There are many stores whose garden departments stock a variety of outdoor lamps but home-made lights are fun to make. They are a challenge to personal ingenuity and the result is often more dreamy and romantic than the harsh light from electric lightbulbs.

Basically two types of light are needed: a neutral white light for checking the food on the grill and warm coloured lights for the dining area.

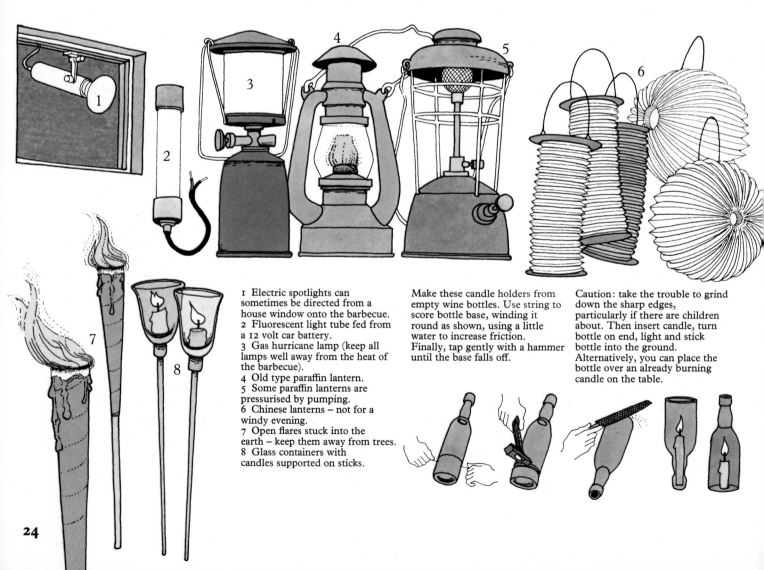

1 Electric spotlights can sometimes be directed from a house window onto the barbecue.
2 Fluorescent light tube fed from a 12 volt car battery.
3 Gas hurricane lamp (keep all lamps well away from the heat of the barbecue).
4 Old type paraffin lantern.
5 Some paraffin lanterns are pressurised by pumping.
6 Chinese lanterns – not for a windy evening.
7 Open flares stuck into the earth – keep them away from trees.
8 Glass containers with candles supported on sticks.

Make these candle holders from empty wine bottles. Use string to score bottle base, winding it round as shown, using a little water to increase friction. Finally, tap gently with a hammer until the base falls off.

Caution: take the trouble to grind down the sharp edges, particularly if there are children about. Then insert candle, turn bottle on end, light and stick bottle into the ground. Alternatively, you can place the bottle over an already burning candle on the table.

Choosing and serving wine

Some grills such as spare ribs call for a drink that can match their spicy flavour and a red vermouth such as Cinzano or Martini rosso does so perfectly. But the smokiness of most other grills needs a drink that blends rather than competes – it needs and wants wine.

Wine is made from the juice of grapes whose sugar has fermented and become alcohol. Wine may contain 8-14 per cent alcohol but its character comes from the soil in which it grew, the type of plant it is, and the art of the vintner who nursed it through its infancy.

The demand for table wines has grown steadily over the past 30 years and pressures of profit and marketing have resulted in large wholesale combines. Since their wines have to stay the same every year to warrant marketing and re-ordering, these wines are usually blended to achieve 'product-continuity' and often carry brand names rather than descriptions of origin.

Some of these wines are good enough for everyday drinking but when they are bought at a supermarket or grocery store it is as well to see first how they are stored. If wine bottles stand upright on shelves their corks dry out and air and bacteria enter and ruin the wine.

Nor should wine be stored in bright sunlight or near radiators since fluctuations of day/night temperatures soon reduce its quality and may turn it into vinegar.

A fine or great wine is best bought from a wine merchant or wine store – from a specialist. It is worthwhile to listen to him and learn; if he is good, he'll love to pass his knowledge on. Wine labels are another source of information and a regular study of their less obvious meanings will soon reveal many delightful secrets.

A wine that has been made and bottled in the country of origin will say so on its label and local regulations are some form of guarantee. Many wines however, are exported in bulk and bottled on arrival and although they carry the legend *Apellation Controlée*, the term has no legal meaning outside the country of origin and the quality depends on the skill of the importer.

There is only one way, and very nice it is too, to find out which wine you like best, and that is to drink it. And if you have found one which you enjoy, hope and pray that your merchant has more of the same.

It is a good idea to keep a wine diary and record the year, the origin, the price and – by allocating a number of stars – the satisfaction a wine has given. Such a record will be more reliable than mere memory of past vintages. Also, since the tastes of no two people are alike, a second column for the remarks of other members of the family or guests is useful when it comes to choosing wine that suits everybody, or for a special birthday lunch or anniversary dinner.

In days gone by, meals were decided on first and the wine chosen confidently afterwards from a wine list that might have more than two hundred entries. But circumstances change and today really good wine is rare, so if a promising bottle has been found it is better to plan the meal around the wine.

Wine can be drunk with anything but some rules are based on common sense. For instance, if more than one type of wine is to be served it is better to follow a poor wine with a fine one and a light wine with a heavy one. Also, red wines are considered not to go well with barbecued fish but are the very drink to serve with steaks and well hung poultry. Red wines are best served at a little above room temperature and if the bottle is stood upright the night before, the sediment will sink to the bottom. Opening it an hour or two before drinking gets rid of the 'bottle-stink' and activates its bouquet.

Dry French white, Rhine or Moselle wines compliment smoked, grilled or shellfish gloriously while sweet wines such as Sauternes seem to go well with desserts. White wines are usually chilled but not frozen as are sparkling and fortified wines excepting port whose serving temperature is optional.

Any wine will go with cheese.

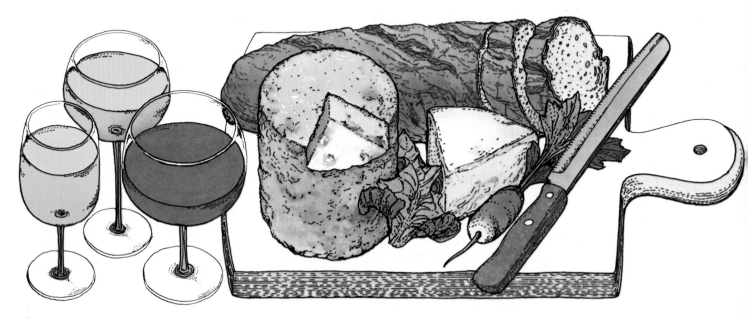

Now and then an unpleasing wine is bought by mistake and to overcome the disappointment, here are two ways to make the best of it. On cool evenings, a mulled wine soon spreads a warm glow to the toes and to the head.

GLÜHWEIN
makes about 6 glasses

1 bottle of red wine
12 cubes of sugar
6 cloves
1 cinnamon stick about 2 in (5 cm)
1 small lemon
1 5 in (12 cm) square of fine white cotton cloth, and
    some thin string

Clean and grate lemon rind finely, crush cloves and cinnamon and place them all in the centre of the cotton. Gather corners of cotton square and tie them together leaving a length of string attached. Pour wine and sugar into saucepan, hang cotton sachet in wine, warm gently and stir but do not boil. Serve in warmed glasses.

On warm summer days, a punchbowl of white wine is not only deliciously cool but also has a strong kick that will make friends of strangers in no time and make a party go with a swing.

SUMMER SPARKLE
makes about 10 glasses

1 bottle dry or medium white wine
1 bottle 17 fl oz (425 ml) lemonade
2 tablespoons (2 × 15 ml) Maraschino or Cointreau
1 lemon
6 borage leaves

Pour wine, lemonade and liqueur into a bowl or jug. Thinly slice the lemon, add and stir. Wash the borage leaves and add. Cool the mixture in a refrigerator for one hour. Serve with small ice cubes.

Try this recipe at least once in your life. It is a meaningful affair that fires the imagination, just right for a chilly evening inside or out, but watch out for hobgoblins and elves that may be attracted by this witches' brew.

HELLFIRE PUNCH
makes about 12 glasses

2 bottles of red table wine
20 lumps of cube sugar
1 orange with 8 cloves inserted
$\frac{1}{2}$ teaspoon (2.5 ml) of cinnamon
$\frac{1}{2}$ teaspoon (2.5 ml) of nutmeg
1 tennisball-sized piece of lump sugar
$\frac{1}{4}$ bottle cognac (at least)

Warm the wine and all other ingredients except cognac and lump sugar in a copper or aluminium pan. Stir gently and keep temperature well below boiling. Bring vessel to the table and use long tongs to hold the piece of lump sugar over the wine. Another of the party then pours some cognac over the sugar and a third sets fire to it. Repeat at intervals. As the blue flame slowly consumes the sugar, thick drops of it fall sizzling into the wine, imparting a spicy flavour to the brew. Serve in warmed glasses.

Let your garden contribute

Whether you measure your garden in acres or flowerpot-inches, home-grown herbs add flavour to a barbecue and are on the whole very easy to grow.

Most herbs originate from the Mediterranean coast and like plenty of sun and shelter from the wind.

They grow in most types of soil, which need not be rich, so peat or leaf mould is better than manure. For very poor soil, apply a general purpose fertilizer at the rate of 4 oz (100 g) per square metre and rake it in.

Most herbs, except mint, grow best in well drained soils and dislike waterlogged conditions. When growing plants in window boxes, use a good potting compost. Take cuttings, sow seeds or transplant the herbs into pots for a winter supply.

Herb	Type	Description	Uses
BALM	*perennial*	Lemon scented. Divide established plants in autumn or sow seeds in spring.	For drinks, poultry dishes, sauces and marinades.
BAY	*evergreen shrub or tree*	Spicy flavour. Take heel cuttings in April. A good container plant.	For flavouring fish and marinades.
BORAGE	*annual*	Cucumber flavour. For winter use, sow seeds in pots in September.	Drinks and salads.
CHERVIL	*biennial*	Ferny leaves with peppery parsley-like flavour. Sow seeds in pots in August for September-October use.	For salads and sauces.
CHIVES	*perennial bulbs*	Onion flavour. Sow seeds in spring. Divide clumps in autumn and pot up for winter use.	For salads, baked potatoes and butters.
DILL	*annual*	Piquant flavour. Sow in July for an autumn supply. Self sown plants are stronger than their parents.	For salads, fish and vegetables.
FENNEL	*perennial*	Aniseed flavour. For winter use transplant into pots.	For fish or garnishing salads.
GARLIC	*annual*	Use a new site every year. Plant the cloves in mid-February, March.	Garlic is garlic! Use sparingly with salads, meats and marinades.
MINT	*perennial*	Common mint, Eau de Cologne, Apple mint or Pepper mint. Watch out for creeping roots. Propagate by root division.	For salads, lamb, potatoes and drinks.
PARSLEY	*annual-biennial*	Has curly leaves. To speed germination, pour boiling water along a shallow trench, sow seeds in it and cover. Sow in July in 5 in pots for winter use.	Use it with meat, poultry, fish and salads. It is rich in vitamin C.
ROSEMARY	*evergreen shrub*	Strongly aromatic. Plant in spring. Take cuttings in March or August.	For beef, pork, lamb, veal and poultry.
SAGE	*evergreen shrub*	Aromatic. Protect in severe winter. Grow from seed in late April. Take 3 in cuttings in August.	For pork and bacon.
SAVORY	*annual (summer)*	Strongly aromatic. Sow seeds in April.	Flavours beans, salads and fish.
TARRAGON	*evergreen perennial*	Plant in spring or September. Increase by division in spring. Tender.	Tarragon vinegar, savoury dishes, chicken.
THYME	*evergreen shrub*	Highly aromatic. Take 2 in cuttings in early summer and plant out in September or pot up for winter use. Pieces can be pegged down, roots will form then sever from main plant and grow on.	For meat, chicken and marinades. Throw thyme leaves onto coals near the end of cooking for flavour.
OAK	*tree*	Leaves, dried. Sawn branches, twigs, wood chips and sawdust.	For smoke-cooking and smoke-curing.
APPLE PEAR PLUM	*fruit trees*	Sawn wood and twigs.	For smoke-cooking and -curing.

Avoid pine or other resinous trees since they will ruin the taste of the food.

table   barbecue   retaining wall

mint

mint

parsley

savory   chives

chervil   garlic   balm

thyme

bay   borage   tarragon   rosemary

sage   fennel   dill

recipes

Most simple barbecues have two grill or firegrate positions but their heat can be varied further by the amount of charcoal used and by leaving the ashes on or knocking them off occasionally. Also grills are usually hotter towards the back and less so near the front where the air enters. The following recipes therefore mention cooking methods that are split roughly into three grades of heat: hot, medium and low.

A simple method of finding the heat of your barbecue is to count the seconds you can comfortably hold your hand over the grill, reciting 'one thousand, two thousand' and so on. If you can count no more than up to 'two thousand' you have a hot fire, up to 'four thousand' is a medium one and up to 'five thousand' or 'six thousand' means that you have a low one.

When cooking in the smoke-oven, temperatures have to be more accurate and you'll need to use a thermometer. Use the conversion scale on page 79 to change Fahrenheit into Centigrade or vice versa.

Beef

Charcoal-grilled beef is one of the greatest specialities that can be cooked on a barbecue. The meat acquires a special taste from the charcoal as if by magic, and somehow its robust flavour makes it the perfect food for eating out of doors. Yet little expertise is needed to barbecue beef successfully – rare, medium or well done portions can be produced simultaneously to suit individual tastes.

Very lean meat like chuck steak is liable to be tough and lacking in flavour. It calls for special treatment such as marinading or preparation with a meat tenderizer and it needs relatively long slow cooking. So if you want to keep things simple, buy steaks mottled with small streaks of fat which are usually the tenderest. The meat should be bright red with a brownish tinge and firm to the touch.

Take the meat out of a refrigerator or freezer in good time to allow it to reach room temperature. Then trim off excess fat and make slashes along the edges of the remaining fat as this helps to prevent the steaks from curling during cooking.

Always grease the grill before cooking. Either brush it with a little oil, or spear a piece of the trimmed-off fat or streaky bacon with a long-handled fork and rub it over the grill. Do not salt uncooked meat as this tends to draw out the juices: your guests will appreciate being allowed to salt the cooked food to their own taste.

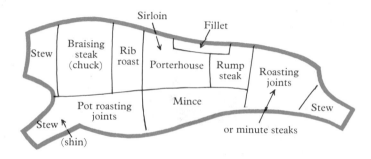

Sear the steaks over hot coals as this seals in the juices, then continue to cook as indicated in the following recipes. Turn only once. If they do start to burn, slip a piece of foil under the steaks and continue to cook. When bubbles appear on the meat's surface, it is time to turn the steaks over. Flip them with tongs rather than a fork since pierced meat will lose valuable juices. The second side will then probably need a little less cooking than the first.

Bon appetit!

STEAK AU POIVRE
Serves 4

4 steaks about 1 in (2.5 cm) thick
4 tablespoons (4 × 15 ml) brandy
2 tablespoons (2 × 15 ml) black peppercorns
2 oz (50 g) butter or margarine
Pinch of oregano or sweet basil
Pinch of garlic salt
2–3 tomatoes

Coarsely crush the peppercorns with a rolling pin and press into both sides of the steaks, then leave them for half an hour. Barbecue over hot coals for about 5–6 minutes each side, then transfer to a hot dish and keep warm. Thickly slice the tomatoes and sauté in the butter in a heavy frying pan over the barbecue coals until they are hot. Sprinkle them with oregano or basil and the garlic salt then arrange them on top of the steaks. Warm the brandy, ignite it with a taper from the barbecue and spoon it flaming over the steaks. Serve immediately.

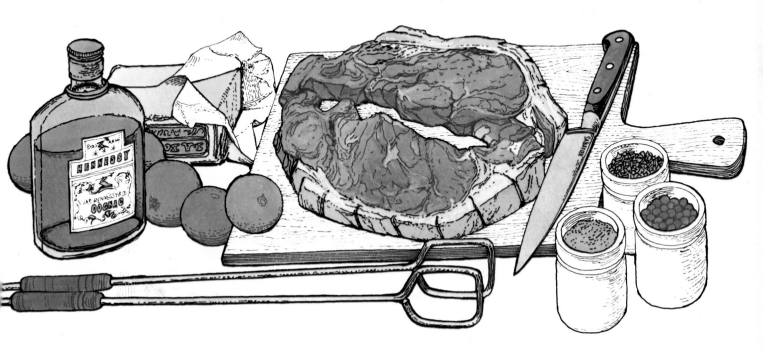

GARLIC STEAKS

Serves 4

4 steaks about 1 in (2.5 cm) thick
4 oz (100 g) butter
1 tablespoon (1 × 15 ml) chopped parsley
Juice of 1 small lemon
1 tablespoon (1 × 15 ml) Worcestershire sauce
3 cloves of garlic
Salt and freshly ground black pepper
French bread

Slash along the fat edges of the steaks to prevent them from curling, then cut one clove of garlic in half and rub over the meat surfaces. Put to one side. Make the garlic butter by beating together the butter, 2 cloves of minced garlic, the parsley, lemon juice, seasoning and Worcestershire sauce. When it is well mixed shape into a log, cover and chill until required. Brush the steaks with a little oil or melted butter and barbecue over hot coals according to taste. When cooked, place a pat of garlic butter on each steak and serve with, or on chunks of French bread.

HERBED STEAKS

Cook as for garlic steaks and when the meat is ready, top it with a pat of herb butter (see page 68).

ONION STEAKS

Cook as for garlic steaks and when the meat is ready, top it with a pat of onion butter (see page 68).

STEAKS WITH GARLIC AND SOUR CREAM

Serves 4

4 steaks about 1 in (2.5 cm) thick
1 carton of sour cream
1 teaspoon (1 × 5 ml) lemon juice
1 teaspoon (1 × 5 ml) Worcestershire sauce
¾ teaspoon (4 ml) freshly ground black pepper
¾ teaspoon (4 ml) celery salt
½ teaspoon (2.5 ml) salt
½ teaspoon (2.5 ml) paprika
2 cloves of garlic, crushed

Mix together all the ingredients. Place the steaks in a shallow dish and pour over the cream, seeing that they are well coated. Cover and leave overnight. Barbecue over hot coals for about 5–6 minutes each side.

Note: Remember to take the steaks out of the refrigerator in good time to allow them to warm up to room temperature before barbecuing.

CHEESE-TOPPED STEAKS

Serves 4

4 small steaks ½ in (1 cm) thick
1 tablespoon (1 × 15 ml) olive or salad oil
1 tablespoon (1 × 15 ml) lemon juice
4 thin slices of cheese
4 soft rolls or chunks of French bread
Pinch of rosemary, oregano, basil or mixed herbs

Mix together the oil and lemon juice and brush it onto the steaks on both sides. Barbecue over hot coals for about 3–4 minutes or longer if you want them well done. Turn, sprinkle with the chosen herbs then place a slice of cheese on top of each steak. While the steaks are cooking, split and toast the rolls on the grill, butter them and sandwich the steaks; or place the steaks on chunks of French bread.

STEAK TERIYAKI

Serves 4–5

1½ lb (675 g) sirloin steak
4 tablespoons (4 × 15 ml) soy sauce
4 tablespoons (4 × 15 ml) brown sugar
3 tablespoons (3 × 15 ml) dry sherry
2 tablespoons (2 × 15 ml) olive or salad oil
1 teaspoon (1 × 5 ml) freshly grated root ginger
or ½ teaspoon (2.5 ml) ground ginger
½ teaspoon (2.5 ml) monosodium glutamate
1–2 cloves of garlic, crushed or finely minced

Cut the steak into ¼ in (6 mm) thick and about 1 in (2.5 cm) wide strips. Mix together the remaining ingredients, then add the steak strips, seeing they are well coated with the mixture. Cover and leave to marinade for 1–2 hours. Drain the strips and weave them onto skewers. Barbecue over hot coals for about 10 minutes, turning often and basting well with the marinade.

Next time, open and drain a small can of water chestnuts placing one at each end of a skewer, or cut 4–5 large tomatoes in half, brush the cut surfaces with French dressing and barbecue for 10 minutes without turning.

SOY AND LIME STEAKS

Serves 4

4 steaks about 1 in (2.5 cm) thick
7 fl oz (200 ml) beef stock
4 tablespoons (4 × 15 ml) soy sauce
2 tablespoons (2 × 15 ml) fresh lime juice
1 tablespoon (1 × 15 ml) brown sugar or clear honey
1 small onion finely chopped
or finely chopped spring onions
1 clove of garlic, crushed

Mix together the stock, soy sauce, lime juice, sugar or honey, onion and garlic. Pour over steaks in a shallow bowl and marinade for 1–2 hours. Drain the steaks and barbecue over hot coals according to taste.

STEAK WITH BLUE CHEESE BUTTER

Serves 4–6

1½ lb (675 g) whole flank steak
6 tablespoons (6 × 15 ml) blue cheese
4 tablespoons (4 × 15 ml) butter or margarine
2 tablespoons (2 × 15 ml) brandy (optional)
1 tablespoon (1 × 15 ml) chopped chives, fresh rosemary or basil
Parsley finely chopped
1 clove of garlic, finely minced
½ pint (300 ml) well seasoned French dressing

Place the steaks in a shallow bowl, cover with French dressing and leave to marinade for several hours. To make the cheese butter, cream the butter and cheese until well blended, then add the brandy (optional), chives/rosemary/basil and garlic. Shape into a log, roll in parsley and then wrap in waxed paper or aluminium foil. Refrigerate, but remember to let it warm to room temperature before using. Drain the steak and barbecue over hot coals for about 5 minutes each side according to whether you like it rare, medium or well done. (If your guests have different tastes, sear the meat over hot coals then slice and cook to individual requirements.) Then cut the meat diagonally into ¼ in (6 mm) slices and place a pat of blue cheese butter on each.

BASIC HAMBURGERS
Serves 6

1½ lb (675 g) best quality medium- or coarse-minced
  beef
1 lightly beaten egg
1 onion finely chopped
1 teaspoon (1 × 5 ml) salt
Dash of freshly ground black pepper
¼ teaspoon (1.2 ml) monosodium glutamate
  (optional)
6 soft rolls

In a bowl *lightly* mix all the ingredients, except the
rolls, together and shape into six ½ in (1 cm) thick
patties. A good tip is to cut six pieces of waxed paper
and to stack the burgers with paper in between which
can later be peeled off when placed on the grill.
Barbecue over hot coals for about 8-10 minutes on
each side. Just before the burgers have finished cooking, split and toast the rolls: serve immediately with
the meat in between the halved rolls.

BACON AND CHEESE BURGERS
Serves 6

1½ lb (675 g) finely minced beef
6 rashers of bacon
4 tablespoons (4 × 15 ml) grated Cheddar cheese
½ teaspoon (2.5 ml) salt
Dash of freshly ground black pepper
1 small onion finely chopped or grated
6 soft rolls

Lightly mix together the beef, salt, pepper and
onion and shape into six patties. Barbecue them over
hot coals for about 8-10 minutes. At the same time,
place the rashers round the edge of the grill and
barbecue until crisp, then crumble them and keep
on one side. Turn the patties and sprinkle the tops
with the grated cheese and crumbled bacon. Cook
for a further 6-8 minutes. Split and toast the rolls
during the last few minutes and serve as usual.

SOY MARINADED HAMBURGERS
Serves 8

3 lb (1½ k) minced beef
7 tablespoons (7 × 15 ml) soy sauce
6 tablespoons (6 × 15 ml) water
6 tablespoons (6 × 15 ml) brown sugar
2 tablespoons (2 × 15 ml) Worcestershire sauce
2 teaspoons (2 × 5 ml) freshly grated root ginger
or 1 teaspoon (1 × 5 ml) ground ginger
8 long rolls
4 thinly sliced tomatoes
1 thinly sliced green pepper

Mix together the soy sauce, water, brown sugar,
Worcestershire sauce and ginger. Divide the mixture
into eight log-shaped patties to fit the rolls. Pour the
marinade over the patties, cover and leave for 1-2
hours. Barbecue over hot coals for about 6-8 minutes,
basting and turning once only. Split and toast the
rolls on the barbecue, then fill each with a meat patty
topped with slices of tomato and green pepper.

Note: If you have a portable barbecue, this is a
good picnic recipe as the meat can be transported in a
tightly sealed bowl and cooked on the spot.

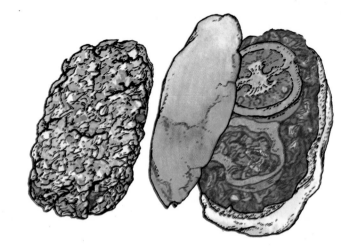

Lamb

The dry heat of charcoal makes lamb particularly succulent and tender and it is usually cooked to medium-rare, when it turns crusty brown on the outside, but remains pink and juicy inside.

Choose the lean, pink meat of young lamb rather than the dark red meat of a mature animal. A useful guide is the colour of the fat: creamy white in spring and summer indicates home produced lamb; white fat means that the animal has been imported. But do not buy meat that has yellowish and brittle fat since this is a sign that the meat is either old or has spent a long time in the freezer.

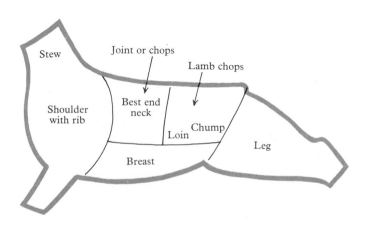

LAMB CHOPS WITH ROSEMARY OR OREGANO
Serves 4

4–8 lamb chops about 1 in (2.5 cm) thick
1–2 tablespoons (1–2 × 15 ml) lemon juice
1–2 teaspoons (1–2 × 5 ml) fresh or dried rosemary or oregano

Slash along the fat edges to prevent the chops from curling, then sprinkle them with lemon juice and either herb. Leave to one side for 30 minutes. Barbecue over medium heat for about 6–8 minutes each side.

MINTED LAMB CHOPS
Cook as for lamb chops with rosemary or oregano and when the chops are ready top with a pat of mint butter (see page 68).

GARLIC CHOPS
Cook as for lamb chops with rosemary or oregano and when the chops are ready top with a pat of garlic butter (see page 67).

MIXED HERB CHOPS
Cook as for lamb chops with rosemary or oregano and when the chops are ready top with a pat of mixed herb butter (see page 68).

SPICED LAMB CHOPS
Serves 4

4 loin, shoulder or thick lamb chops
2 teaspoons (2 × 5 ml) ground coriander seed
1 teaspoon (1 × 5 ml) chilli powder
½ teaspoon (2.5 ml) ground cummin seed
1 clove of garlic, crushed
A little vinegar
Salt

In a bowl mix all the ingredients (not salt) with a little vinegar to make a paste. Rub well onto both sides of the chops and leave for about 30 minutes. Place on an oiled grill and barbecue over medium heat for about 6–8 minutes. When ready sprinkle with a little salt and serve immediately.

SMOKE-COOKED LEG OF LAMB
Serves 8

4½ lb (2 kg) leg of lamb, boned, rolled and tied
6 tablespoons (6 × 15 ml) sherry or orange juice
4 tablespoons (4 × 15 ml) chopped fresh mint leaves
2 tablespoons (2 × 15 ml) olive or salad oil
1 dessertspoon (1 × 10 ml) salt
1 teaspoon (1 × 5 ml) oregano or tarragon
½ teaspoon (2.5 ml) freshly ground black pepper
1 medium onion, grated
Fresh mint leaves

Mix together all the ingredients and rub the mixture evenly over the leg of lamb. Place in a dish, cover and leave for about 8 hours. Arrange the glowing charcoals round the edge of the fire-base and place a water filled drip pan under the roasting area. Place the meat on the grill, cover with a hood or one made of foil and cook in medium heat for about 2¼–3 hours. Every 30 minutes throw a handful of mint leaves onto the coals, adding additional charcoals if needed to maintain even heat.

CHEESE TOPPED LAMB CHOPS
Serves 3

6 lamb chops 1 in (2.5 cm) thick
2 tablespoons (2 × 15 ml) butter
2 oz (50 g) grated Parmesan cheese
Dash of salt and freshly ground black pepper

Mix together the butter, cheese, salt and pepper. Trim excess fat and slash along the remaining fat edges of the chops. Barbecue over medium heat for about 6–8 minutes. Turn and continue to cook for a further 4 minutes then spread the cheese mixture over the top of the chops and continue to barbecue for a further 2 minutes.

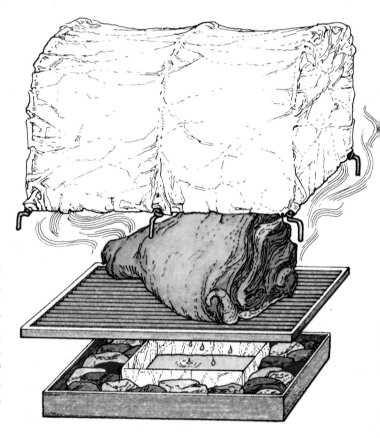

Pork

Pork is a rich meat the taste of which can be enhanced by the smoky barbecue flavour. Large cuts need barbecuing for many hours, so to reduce the cooking time it is better to buy smaller cuts. Choose young pork which has a fine texture and a pink colour, rather than meat from older animals which is coarser in texture and darker in colour. All pork however requires slow barbecuing over low to medium heat and when cooked the meat should no longer be pink, but almost cream in colour. Always ensure that pork is cooked thoroughly inside.

Smoke-cooking of pork is also possible and is done under a hood as described on page 11, while marinading adds further dimensions to the taste of the meat.

Pork spareribs are one of the barbecue specials; they can be eaten cave-man style, held with the fingers so that every little piece of the smoky, mouth-watering meat can be gnawed. Ordinarily, spareribs have very little meat between the bones – a meatier meal can be had by buying loin back ribs or chump sparerib chops.

Barbecued meat is just as delicious when eaten cold, so it is worthwhile to barbecue an extra chop or two for nibbling the next day.

FOILED PORK CHOPS WITH APPLE
Serves 1

1 pork chop, 1 in (2.5 cm) thick, fat edges slashed
1 small cooking apple
1 tablespoon (1 × 15 ml) butter or margarine
1 dessertspoon (1 × 10 ml) brown sugar
Dash of salt and pepper

Wash and core the apple then cut into $\frac{1}{2}$ in (1.5 cm) rings. Place a lightly seasoned pork chop in the centre of a square of greased foil. Top with the apple rings, dot with knobs of butter, then sprinkle the surface with the brown sugar. Wrap firmly, seeing that the edges are well sealed, and barbecue over hot coals for 1 hour, turning often.

Note : If the bone ends are sharp, wrap these with small pieces of foil before placing in the larger sheet of foil.

Joint or chops

Spare ribs

Boneless pork roast

Pork chops

Belly slices

Best end or cutlet

Half leg knuckle

BARBECUED PORK CHOPS
Serves 6

6 loin or chump pork chops cut 1 in (2.5 cm) thick
8 fl oz (200 ml) water
6 fl oz (150 ml) tomato ketchup
2 fl oz (50 ml) olive or salad oil
2 fl oz (50 ml) lemon juice
3 tablespoons (3 × 15 ml) brown sugar
2 tablespoons (2 × 15 ml) Worcestershire sauce
1 dessertspoon (1 × 10 ml) prepared mustard
2 teaspoons (2 × 5 ml) salt
Dash of Tabasco sauce
2 medium onions, chopped
1 clove of garlic, minced

In a pan, heat the oil until hot then add the onions and garlic, cooking them until they are tender but not brown. Add the ketchup, water, lemon juice, sugar, Worcestershire sauce, mustard and Tabasco sauce. Bring to the boil and then simmer, uncovered, for 15 minutes. Leave to cool. Slash the fat edges of the chops and barbecue them over low heat turning every 10–15 minutes for about an hour. During the last 20 minutes of barbecuing, baste frequently with the sauce.

For additional flavour, try tossing a sprig of rosemary, lemon thyme or a couple of bay leaves onto the burning coals just before the meat is almost cooked.

HONEY GLAZED HAM
Serves 6-8

A 2 lb (900 g) tin of ham
9 tablespoons (9 × 15 ml) clear honey
2 teaspoons (2 × 5 ml) cinnamon

Mix together the honey and cinnamon. Open the tin of ham and scrape off any aspic jelly. Barbecue the ham over medium coals for about 45 minutes or until thoroughly heated, turning and basting frequently with the honey glaze.

FOILED HAM AND PINEAPPLE
Serves 1

1 slice of cooked ham, 1 in (2.5 cm) thick
1 pineapple ring
1 tablespoon (1 × 15 ml) brown sugar
½ teaspoon (2.5 ml) prepared mustard
1 clove
Butter or margarine

Stick the clove into the pineapple ring. Place the ham slice in the middle of a piece of greased foil. Spread the mustard over the ham, then sprinkle it with the brown sugar. Top with the pineapple ring and dot with knobs of butter. Wrap firmly, seeing that the edges are well sealed. Barbecue over hot coals, turning once, for about 30 minutes.

SPARERIBS TERIYAKI
Serves 4

4 chump, loin or sparerib chops about 1 in (2.5 cm) thick
4 tablespoons (4 × 15 ml) soy sauce
2 tablespoons (2 × 15 ml) clear honey
2 tablespoons (2 × 15 ml) salad or olive oil
1 tablespoon (1 × 15 ml) red wine vinegar
1 teaspoon (1 × 5 ml) freshly grated root ginger
or ½ teaspoon (2.5 ml) ground ginger
1–2 cloves of garlic, crushed

Mix together all the ingredients and spoon over the chops. Cover and leave to marinade for about 4 hours before barbecuing, turning occasionally. Drain the chops and barbecue over low heat for about 40 minutes, turning and basting the chops every 10–15 minutes.

Poultry

Poultry is very popular for barbecues because it can be cooked in a variety of ways; straight on the grill, marinaded, smoke-cooked and smoke-cured. However, while chicken and turkey are fairly dry meats and can be placed straight on the grill, duck and goose contain a lot of fat, take longer to cook, and need to be cooked over a drip pan as described on page 11.

Whole birds need to be barbecued on a spit, but as this can take several hours, it is often more convenient either to barbecue a small bird cut in half lengthways or to barbecue pieces. When barbecuing chicken for a large party, it is also more economical to buy pieces rather than whole birds.

Turkey drumsticks can be barbecued in the same way as chicken pieces, directly on the grill or in a hinged wire basket. To barbecue duck pieces, prick them all over with a fork to release the fat – do not baste them.

When the pieces of poultry are ready, they should be light brown and crisp on the outside, tender and juicy inside. The juices should be clear and should sizzle on the surface, but with poultry that has been frozen it is always advisable to guard against food poisoning by checking that the meat is cooked right through to the middle.

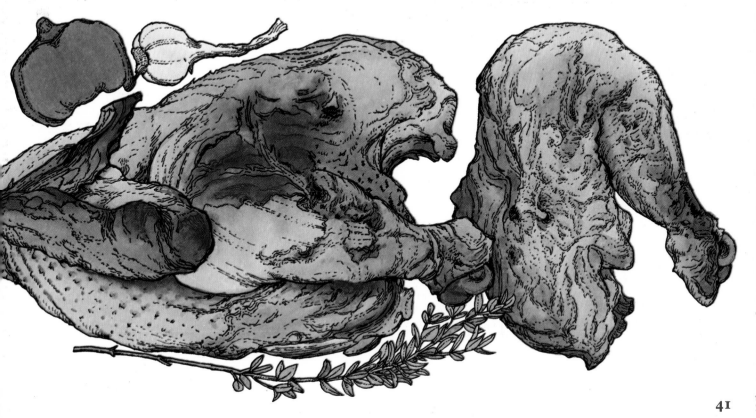

TANDOORI MURGHA (Indian)
Serves 4-6

3½ lb (1¾ k) chicken cut into joints or 4-6 chicken
  pieces
2 cloves of garlic, minced
1 medium onion, finely chopped or grated
5 fl oz (150 ml) plain yogurt
1 teaspoon (1 × 5 ml) ground coriander
1 teaspoon (1 × 5 ml) garam masala
1 teaspoon (1 × 5 ml) chilli powder
1 teaspoon (1 × 5 ml) ground ginger
2-3 oz (50-75 g) butter
Lemon juice
Salt and freshly ground black pepper
Red colouring – cochineal

Skin the chicken pieces, prick with a fork and lightly season. In a bowl, mix together the coriander, garam masala, chilli powder, ginger and a few drops of cochineal. Add the onion, garlic and yogurt and enough lemon juice to make a thick paste. Gash the flesh and rub the paste all over the chicken pieces. Cover and leave to marinade for 4-6 hours or over-night. Place the chicken pieces on the grill and bar-becue over medium heat for about 40 minutes or until tender. After 10 minutes, brush with melted butter and continue cooking, turning, and basting with the butter occasionally.

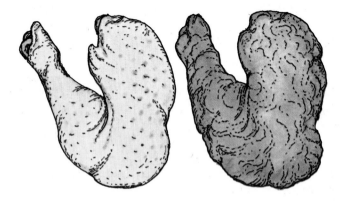

LEMON CHICKEN HALVES
Serves 4

2 small chickens split in half lengthways
4 oz (100 g) butter or margarine
2 tablespoons (2 × 15 ml) lemon juice
½ teaspoon (2.5 ml) garlic salt
Dash of freshly ground white pepper
A spiral of orange or lemon peel (optional)

Wash the chicken halves and pat them dry. Melt the butter or margarine and add the lemon juice, garlic salt and white pepper. Lightly season both sides of the chicken halves and place on the grill, bone sides down. Brush with the mixture and barbecue over medium heat for about 20 minutes. Turn, brush again with the mixture and continue to cook for a further 20 minutes or until tender. 5 minutes before the end of cooking, throw the spiral of peel onto the barbecue coals – the aroma is fabulous.

For a change, peel, cut and stone two large peaches to go with the chicken. Brush them with marinade and barbecue for about 5 minutes on each side.

HERBED CHICKEN BREASTS
Serves 6-8

6-8 large boned chicken breasts
8 oz (200 g) butter
6 oz (150 g) seasoned flour
1 teaspoon (1 × 5 ml) olive or salad oil
1 teaspoon (1 × 5 ml) crushed dried herbs

Wash the chicken breasts and pat them dry. Mix together the herbs and the seasoned flour and put them into a large plastic bag. Melt three quarters of the butter and add the oil, then dip a breast into this, and place it in the bag containing flour and herbs. Shake well, seeing that the breast is well coated. Repeat this procedure for the remaining breasts. Barbecue the breasts over hot coals for about 10 minutes each side, basting frequently with the re-maining 2 oz (50 g) of melted butter.

FOILED CHICKEN AND VEGETABLES
Serves 1

1 chicken piece
1 oz (25 g) butter or margarine
1 small potato
1 tomato
1 medium onion
2 green or red pepper rings
2 mushrooms
Worcestershire sauce
Dash of salt and freshly ground black pepper

Peel the onion and cut into rings. Wash the potato, mushrooms, tomato and green or red pepper before cutting them into slices. Wash and pat dry the chicken piece then place it in the centre of a square of greased foil. Cover with the vegetable slices, a few drops of Worcestershire sauce, season lightly and dot with butter. Wrap firmly seeing that the edges are well sealed. Barbecue over hot coals for 40-50 minutes, turning often. To accompany the chicken try garlic, onion or herb bread (page 67) – use it to mop up all those delicious juices.

PAPRIKA CHICKEN
Serves 4-6

4-6 chicken joints
6 tablespoons (6 × 15 ml) olive or salad oil
2 tablespoons (2 × 15 ml) tarragon vinegar
1 teaspoon (1 × 5 ml) paprika
1 teaspoon (1 × 5 ml) sugar
½ teaspoon (2.5 ml) salt
½ teaspoon (2.5 ml) freshly ground black pepper
1-2 cloves of garlic, crushed

Mix together all the ingredients in a jar with a lid, shake well and leave for an hour or so. Wash the chicken pieces and pat them dry. Brush them with the mixture and barbecue over medium heat for about 40 minutes or until tender, turning and basting with the mixture frequently, until well browned.

HEARTY CHICKEN HALVES
Serves 6

3 small chickens, split in half lengthways or 6
    frozen chicken halves
8 fl oz (200 ml) sherry or apple juice
4 fl oz (100 ml) olive or salad oil
1 tablespoon (1 × 15 ml) prepared mustard
1 tablespoon (1 × 15 ml) Worcestershire sauce
1 tablespoon (1 × 15 ml) mixed herbs
1 teaspoon (1 × 5 ml) soy sauce
1 teaspoon (1 × 5 ml) garlic salt
½ teaspoon (2.5 ml) salt
¼ teaspoon (1.2 ml) freshly ground pepper
1 large onion, grated

In a bowl mix together all the ingredients. Wash the chicken halves and pat them dry. Place them in the bottom of a shallow dish and pour the marinade over them. Cover and refrigerate for about 4 hours, turning the halves occasionally. Drain the pieces and place them bone side down on the grill. Barbecue over medium heat for about 20-30 minutes, basting frequently. Turn and continue to cook and baste for a further 30 minutes or until tender.

Note: If using frozen chicken halves, see that they are well thawed before using.

HONEY GLAZED CHICKEN
Serves 4

4 chicken joints
6 tablespoons (6 × 15 ml) clear honey
3 tablespoons (3 × 15 ml) ready mixed mustard
2 tablespoons (2 × 15 ml) lemon juice
2 oz (50 g) melted butter
Dash of salt and freshly ground white pepper

Wash the joints and pat them dry. To make the honey glaze, mix together the honey, mustard, lemon juice and seasoning. Lightly season the joints, brush them with the melted butter and barbecue over medium heat, turning and basting frequently, for about 25 minutes. Brush the joints with the honey glaze and continue to barbecue for a further 10–15 minutes, still turning and basting.

SMOKE-COOKED CHICKEN
Serves 3–4

1 fresh chicken, weighing 3 lb (1.3 kg)
2–4 rashers of smoked bacon

Rinse the chicken and pat it dry. Set the grill over medium heat. Place the chicken on the grill and two rashers of bacon on top of the chicken. During cooking, place damp pieces or chips of wood on the coals to make smoke. Cover the grill with a hood and adjust the draught so that the fire smoulders and does not burn. Add new and warmed pieces of charcoal to keep the heat constant. When the chicken is good and brown on one side, turn it over and place two more rashers on top. It will be ready after about 1¼ hours.

SMOKE-COOKED POUSSIN
Serves 2 (or 4 as a first course)

2 poussins
6 tablespoons (6 × 15 ml) butter, melted
4 tablespoons (4 × 15 ml) brown sugar
4 tablespoons (4 × 15 ml) lemon juice
4 tablespoons (4 × 15 ml) sherry or brandy
Salt and freshly ground pepper

Mix together the butter, brown sugar, lemon juice and sherry or brandy. Rinse the chickens and pat them dry. Tie the legs together and lightly season the chickens. Place them on the grill, breast side uppermost over a medium fire. Baste with the sauce and cover the grill with a hood. Adjust the draught so that the fire burns without flames, keeping the charcoal to the side of the chickens. Cook for about 45–60 minutes and baste occasionally.

HERB SMOKED POUSSIN
Serves 4

4 poussins
4 oz (50 g) butter
2 tablespoons (2 × 15 ml) chopped chives
½ tablespoon (2.5 ml) crushed rosemary
Salt and freshly ground pepper

Make a herb butter by mixing together the butter, chopped chives and crushed rosemary. Lightly season the chickens inside and out and place 1 tablespoon (15 ml) of herb butter in the large cavity of each bird. Then fasten the cavities with wooden sticks or small skewers. Tie the legs together, and proceed to cook as above, occasionally basting with the herb butter.

Fish

Fish is delicate and falls apart easily, but with care it can be barbecued directly on the open grill, when it should be turned very carefully and only once. A more reliable method is to place it in a hinged wire basket (well oiled), which allows the fish to be turned with less danger of breaking it.

Dry fish needs frequent basting while it is being barbecued, but oily fish should need no basting since it cooks in its own oil. Barbecue small individual fish or fish steaks for 10-15 minutes. Large fish will need 7-9 minutes per pound (500 g).

Another excellent way of barbecuing fish is to wrap it in well greased aluminium foil (shiny surface inside), which seals in the juices, but it is a good idea to open the foil-parcels during the last 5 minutes of cooking on the grill so that the fish absorbs the smoky barbecue flavour. This also allows you to see when the fish is cooked. Foil-wrapped fish require longer cooking times – about 20 per cent more than that of unwrapped fish.

Watch fish carefully since it is ready the moment it can be flaked easily with a fork.

BARBECUED TROUT IN FOIL

Serves 4

4 fresh trout, cleaned
4 oz (100 g) butter
Salt and freshly ground black pepper
Dash of lemon juice
Sprigs of fresh fennel, thyme or tarragon (optional)

If desired, remove the heads then wash the fish quickly, drain and dry carefully. Lightly spread 1 oz (25 g) of butter inside each fish, a dash of lemon juice and then lightly season. Place a few sprigs of fennel, thyme or tarragon in each cavity, before wrapping in greased foil. Barbecue over medium/hot coals, turning only once, for about 30 minutes. Open up the foil during the last 5 minutes to get that really smoky barbecue taste.

GRILLED TROUT WITH ALMONDS

Serves 4

4 fresh trout
6 oz (175 g) butter
4 tablespoons (4 × 15 ml) seasoned flour
2 tablespoons (2 × 15 ml) flaked almonds
3 tablespoons (3 × 15 ml) lemon juice
2 tablespoons (2 × 15 ml) chopped parsley

Cut off the heads, wash and pat the fish dry. Dip them in the seasoned flour and place in an oiled hinged wire basket. Barbecue the fish on one side over hot coals for about 15 minutes or until the fish flakes with a fork. Turn once and cook the other side, basting well with half of the butter (melted). Melt the remaining butter in a saucepan at the side of the grill, add the almonds and allow to brown. Add the lemon juice and parsley. Place fish on warmed plates and pour over the almond sauce. Serve with chunks of French bread.

SALMON TREAT
Serves 4

1½ lb (675 g) salmon steaks
2 tablespoons (2 × 15 ml) lemon juice
½ teaspoon (2.5 ml) dried or fresh rosemary
Salt and freshly ground black pepper
2 fl oz (50 ml) olive or salad oil

In a jar with a lid, mix together the lemon juice, oil and rosemary, shake well and put aside for 2 hours. Strain the mixture and coat the steaks, then sprinkle with a little salt and black pepper. Place the steaks on the grill or in a hinged wire basket and barbecue over medium/hot coals for about 8 minutes. Brush with the mixture and turn. Baste again and continue to cook for a further 8 minutes or until done.

FOILED HALIBUT FILLETS
Serves 1

½ lb (225 g) fresh or frozen halibut fillets
4 tablespoons (4 × 15 ml) grated carrot
4 tablespoons (4 × 15 ml) chopped celery
2 tablespoons (2 × 15 ml) chopped or grated onion
1 tablespoon (1 × 15 ml) butter or margarine
1 teaspoon (1 × 5 ml) lemon juice
½ teaspoon (2.5 ml) salt
¼ teaspoon (1.2 ml) freshly ground pepper, salt and
   paprika

Well grease a 12 in (31 cm) square of double thickness foil. Mix together the ¼ teaspoon (1.2 ml) of pepper, salt, and the paprika and sprinkle over the fillets. Place the vegetables in the middle of the foil, sprinkle with the ½ teaspoon (2.5 ml) salt and then top with the fillets. Dot with knobs of butter and sprinkle with the lemon juice. Wrap securely seeing that the edges are well sealed, and barbecue over medium coals for about 10–12 minutes each side.

Note: If using frozen fillets see that they are well thawed before using.

SPICED HERRINGS IN FOIL
Serves 4

4 large fresh herrings
1 teaspoon (1 × 5 ml) chilli powder
1 teaspoon (1 × 5 ml) garam masala
1 teaspoon (1 × 5 ml) turmeric powder
1 medium onion, grated
1 clove of garlic, crushed
Juice of a lemon
Salt

Wash the herrings and pat them dry, sprinkle with a little salt and leave to one side. Peel and grate the onion. In a bowl mix together the chilli powder, garam masala, turmeric, onion and garlic. Add the lemon juice to make a paste and spread it over the inside and outside of the herrings. Wrap each herring in greased aluminium foil and barbecue over medium heat for about 20 minutes, turning only once. During the last five minutes of cooking, open the foil to allow the fish to absorb the smoky barbecue flavour, and to see if the fish flakes easily with a fork.

SMOKE-COOKED SALMON STEAKS
Serves 6

6 fresh salmon steaks 1 in (2.5 cm) thick
2-2½ lemons
6 tablespoons (6 × 15 ml) butter, melted
1 teaspoon (1 × 5 ml) curry powder or
½ teaspoon (2.5 ml) crushed rosemary
½ teaspoon (2.5 ml) salt
¼ teaspoon (1.2 ml) freshly ground pepper

Make a drip pan out of heavy duty foil large enough to take all the steaks. Cover the base of the pan with thin slices of lemon and place the salmon steaks on top. Mix together the butter and curry powder (or rosemary). Pour the mixture over the steaks and lightly season them. Arrange the charcoal to give a medium heat and place the pan with the steaks on the grill. Cover the grill with a hood and now and then add damp wood chips to produce smoke. Cook for about 45 minutes or until the fish flakes easily with a fork, basting occasionally with the juices from the drip-pan.

Try serving the steaks with a cucumber salad. Peel and slice 3 cucumbers. Mix 10 fl oz (284 ml) of seasoned yoghurt with 2 tablespoons (2 × 15 ml) chopped mint. Pour over cucumber, toss and chill for 20 minutes.

SMOKE-COOKED SALMON FILLET
Serves 2 (or 4 as a first course)

1 lb (450 g) fillet of fresh salmon
Salt and freshly ground pepper
Butter or margarine

Make a drip-pan out of heavy duty aluminium foil, large enough to take the fillet and grease it lightly. Place the fish in the pan and the pan on the grill over low heat and brush the fish with a little melted butter. Cover the grill with a hood and add wood chips to the fire to produce smoke. Grill and smoke for about 2 hours or until the fish flakes easily with a fork. Season lightly before serving.

SMOKE-COOKED FISH STEAKS
Serves 4

4 firm fish steaks 1 in (2.5 cm) thick
4 tablespoons (4 × 15 ml) butter
1 large clove of garlic, minced or crushed
1½ lemons
Salt and freshly ground pepper

Thinly slice the lemons, heat the butter and add the garlic. Make a drip-pan out of heavy-duty foil, large enough to take the steaks. Cover the bottom of the pan with lemon slices and place the fish steaks on top of them. Pour the garlic butter over the steaks and then lightly season them. Place the pan on the grill over low heat and cover the grill with a hood. Baste occasionally with juices from the pan, at the same time adding more charcoal and the odd chip of damp wood to create a smoky flavour. Smoke-cook for about 2 hours or until the fish flakes easily.

Kebabs

Looking like coloured beads on a string, kebabs tickle the taste buds with a succession of different barbecue delights. Meat, poultry, fish, bread and vegetables can all be barbecued on skewers, even fruit and yummy marshmallows. For a party, allow your guests to choose their own combinations.

Always oil skewers before threading the ingredients onto them. Generally, it is a good idea to cut vegetable pieces larger than their accompanying meat cubes so as to compensate for their different cooking speeds.

When barbecuing fish, leave the skin on the pieces and pierce them with the skewer as this helps to prevent the fish from falling apart.

Always baste kebabs with oil, melted butter/margarine or marinades to prevent their drying up. Marinades spice and tenderize the ingredients and any remaining marinade can be served as a sauce with the cooked kebabs.

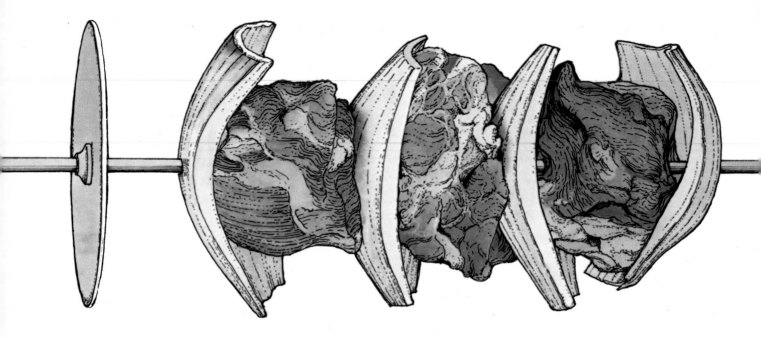

SPICED LAMB KEBABS
Serves 4

1½ lb (675 g) boned leg of lamb
2 teaspoons (2 × 5 ml) ground coriander seed
1 teaspoon (1 × 5 ml) freshly ground black pepper
1 teaspoon (1 × 5 ml) chilli powder
½ teaspoon (2.5 ml) turmeric powder
5 fl oz (150 ml) plain yogurt
6 small onions

Cut and trim the lamb into 1 in (2.5 cm) cubes and place in a bowl. Mix together the spices and yogurt. Add the mixture to the meat, cover and leave to marinade for 4-6 hours, turning occasionally. Cut the onions into quarters and separate the layers. Drain the meat and thread the cubes with the onions onto skewers. Brush each completed skewer with a little oil and barbecue over hot coals for about 15 minutes, turning and basting frequently.

CURRIED LAMB KEBABS
Serves 4

1½ lb (675 g) boned leg of lamb or lamb fillets
4 tablespoons (4 × 15 ml) clear honey
2 tablespoons (2 × 15 ml) lemon juice
2 tablespoons (2 × 15 ml) olive or salad oil
½ teaspoon (2.5 ml) salt
½–1 teaspoon (2.5-5 ml) good curry powder
Dash of freshly ground black pepper
1 green pepper cut into 8 chunks

Trim and cut the meat into 1 in (2.5 cm) cubes. Mix together the honey, lemon juice, oil, salt, curry powder and black pepper. Wash and de-seed the green pepper, then cut into 8 pieces and parboil for 1 minute in salted water. Thread the cubes of lamb and green pepper pieces onto skewers and barbecue over hot coals for about 15 minutes, turning and frequently basting with the mixture.

PRUNE AND LAMB KEBABS
Serves 4-6

2 lb (900 g) lamb fillet or top of leg
4 tablespoons (4 × 15 ml) olive or salad oil
4 tablespoons (4 × 15 ml) lemon juice
2 tablespoons (2 × 15 ml) tomato ketchup
1 teaspoon (1 × 5 ml) soy sauce
½ teaspoon (2.5 ml) Worcestershire sauce
1 teaspoon (1 × 5 ml) freshly grated root ginger
or ½ teaspoon (2.5 ml) ground ginger
Dash of salt and freshly ground black pepper
1 × 7½ oz can (212 g) prunes
2 cloves of garlic, crushed
1 green pepper
12 bay leaves (fresh if possible)
24 button onions

Trim and cut the lamb into bite-sized pieces and place in a bowl. Drain, wash and stone the prunes. Peel the onions, wash and de-seed the green pepper and cut up into largish pieces. Blanch the onions and green pepper in boiling salted water for 5 minutes. Mix together the oil, lemon juice, tomato ketchup, soy sauce, Worcestershire sauce, ginger, seasoning and garlic. Add the mixture to the meat, cover, and leave to marinade for about 2 hours. Thread the meat, onions, prunes, green pepper and bay leaves on to 4 or 6 skewers. Brush each completed skewer with the marinade and barbecue over medium heat for about 15 minutes, turning and basting frequently.

SOUTH AFRICAN SASSATIES
Serves 4

1½ lb (675 g) lamb fillets or top of leg
¼ pint (150 ml) red wine vinegar
4 tablespoons (4 × 15 ml) olive or salad oil
2 tablespoons (2 × 15 ml) brown sugar
2 tablespoons (2 × 15 ml) mango chutney
2 tablespoons (2 × 15 ml) sieved apricot jam
1 tablespoon (1 × 15 ml) curry powder
1 oz (25 g) onion, finely chopped
1-2 cloves of garlic, crushed
8 slices of orange
4 slices of lemon
16 baby onions

Trim and cut the lamb into bite-sized chunks and place them, together with the fruit slices, in a bowl. In a pan mix together the vinegar, oil, brown sugar, chutney, jam, curry powder, onion and crushed garlic. Slowly bring to the boil, stirring continuously until the sugar has dissolved. Simmer for 10 minutes and while still hot pour over the lamb and fruit slices. Cover and leave to marinade overnight. Blanch the baby onions for 5 minutes in boiling salted water until almost tender, drain and add to the lamb. Skewer the meat cubes, fruit slices and onions alternately, starting and ending with an orange slice. Brush the completed skewers with the marinade and barbecue them over medium heat for about 15 minutes, turning and basting frequently.

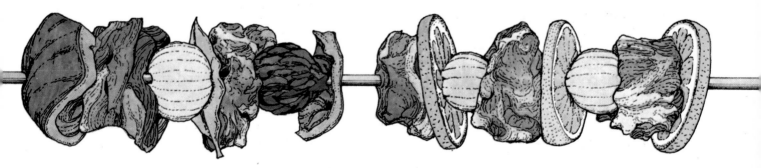

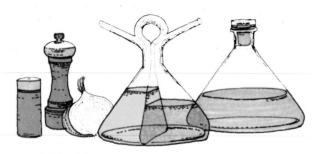

SHISH KEBAB
Serves 4-5

$2\frac{1}{2}$ lb ($1\frac{1}{4}$ kg) top of leg of lamb
4 tablespoons (4 × 15 ml) olive or salad oil
3 tablespoons (3 × 15 ml) dry sherry or red wine
   vinegar
2 tablespoons (2 × 15 ml) lemon juice
2 tablespoons (2 × 15 ml) chopped parsley
1 teaspoon (1 × 5 ml) crushed black peppercorns
$\frac{1}{2}$ teaspoon (2.5 ml) salt
1 teaspoon (1 × 5 ml) dried oregano
1 small onion finely chopped
2 cloves of garlic, crushed
1 bay leaf
4 mushroom caps
4 small tomatoes
2 medium onions, quartered
2 small green peppers

Trim and cut the lamb into 1 in (2.5 cm) cubes and place in a bowl. Mix together the oil, sherry (or vinegar), lemon juice, parsley, pepper, salt, dried oregano, onion, garlic and bay leaf. Pour the mixture over the meat, cover and refrigerate for about 12 hours turning several times. Cut the onions and green peppers into wedges and boil for 4 minutes in salted water. Drain the meat and thread the cubes onto skewers alternating with pepper, onion and mushroom until the skewer is filled leaving enough room to spear a tomato on the end. Brush each completed skewer with marinade and barbecue over hot coals for about 15 minutes, turning and basting frequently.

SWEET-SOUR LAMB KEBABS
Serves 4

$1\frac{1}{2}$ lb (675 g) boned top leg of lamb
1 × 16 oz can (454 g) pineapple cubes
6 oz (150 g) button mushrooms
2 small green peppers
Bay leaves (fresh if possible)
2 tablespoons (2 × 15 ml) brown sugar
2 tablespoons (2 × 15 ml) clear honey
2 tablespoons (2 × 15 ml) red wine vinegar
$\frac{1}{2}$ teaspoon (2.5 ml) dried basil
Dash of salt and freshly ground black pepper

Trim and cut the lamb into 1 in (2.5 cm) cubes and place in a bowl. Wash and de-seed the green peppers and cut into fairly large pieces. Wash the mushrooms. Drain the pineapple cubes and keep the juice. In a pan mix together the brown sugar, honey, vinegar, basil, salt, pepper and pineapple juice. Heat gently stirring continuously until the sugar has dissolved. Bring to the boil, reduce heat and cook for a further minute. Thread the meat, mushrooms, green pepper and bay leaves alternately onto skewers. Brush the kebabs with the mixture and barbecue over medium heat for about 15 minutes, turning and basting frequently.

BACON KEBABS
Serves 4

$1\frac{1}{2}$ lb (675 g) lean bacon – slipper or forehock
2 oz (50 g) butter or margarine
Dash of salt and freshly ground pepper
3 large bananas
8 small tomatoes

Trim the fat and cut the bacon into $\frac{3}{4}$ in (2 cm) cubes. Peel and cut the bananas into 4 or 5 pieces. Thread the bacon, bananas and tomatoes alternately onto skewers. Brush each completed skewer with melted butter and barbecue over medium heat for 15-20 minutes, frequently turning and basting with the melted butter.

FISH KEBABS
Serves 4

2 lb (1 kg) cod or haddock steaks or fillets
2 tablespoons (2 × 15 ml) lemon juice
2 oz (50 g) butter or margarine, melted
Dash of salt and freshly ground pepper
4 tomatoes
1 green pepper

Wash and pat dry the fish, leaving the skin on. Then cut into 1 in (2.5 cm) pieces. Wash and de-seed the green pepper, cut into chunks and boil for 1 minute in salted water. Halve the tomatoes and thread with the fish and pepper pieces onto skewers. Always pierce through the fish skin. Season well with salt and pepper. Add the lemon juice to the melted butter and brush each skewer well. Barbecue over medium heat for 8-10 minutes or until done, turning and basting frequently.

YOGURT BEEF KEBABS
Serves 4-5

1-1½ lb (450-675 g) rump steak about 1 in (2.5 cm) thick
5 fl oz (150 ml) natural yogurt
¼ pint (150 ml) tomato juice
1 tablespoon (1 × 15 ml) onion finely chopped
2 teaspoons (2 × 5 ml) Worcestershire sauce
1 teaspoon (1 × 5 ml) dried sage
½ teaspoon (2.5 ml) dried marjoram
Pinch of cayenne
Salt and freshly ground black pepper
8 mushroom caps
1 green pepper
4 tomatoes

Trim and cut the steak into 1 in (2.5 cm) cubes. Mix together the yogurt, tomato juice, onion, Worcestershire sauce, sage, marjoram, cayenne and a dash of salt and black pepper. Add the meat to the mixture and coat well. Cover and leave to marinade for about 4 hours, turning occasionally. Wash and de-seed the green pepper, cut it into 8 pieces and boil for 1 minute in salted water. Clean the mushrooms and halve the tomatoes. Drain the meat and thread the cubes onto skewers alternating with the mushrooms, green pepper and tomatoes. Barbecue over medium heat for about 20 minutes, turning frequently and basting often.

SOUVLAKIA (Greek Kebabs)
Serves 4-5

2½ lb (1¼ kg) lean lamb
2 tablespoons (2 × 15 ml) olive or salad oil
1 tablespoon (1 × 15 ml) dried oregano
Juice of 1 lemon
2 medium onions, quartered
1 tablespoon (1 × 15 ml) chopped parsley
About 8-10 bay leaves (fresh if possible)
Pinch of salt and freshly ground black pepper

Trim and cut the meat into 1 in (2.5 cm) cubes and place in a bowl. Mix together the oil, oregano, lemon juice, salt, pepper and parsley. Pour the mixture over the meat, cover and marinade for 1-2 hours. Drain the meat and thread the cubes onto skewers, with a bay leaf and a piece of onion. Brush the completed skewers with the marinade and barbecue over hot coals for about 15 minutes, turning frequently and basting with the marinade.

Note : Beef or poultry can also be used with this marinade. Tomatoes and green pepper can be alternated with the meat or poultry.

SATE AYAM (Indonesian)
Serves 4-6

1 lb (450 g) skinned chicken breasts
2 tablespoons (2 × 15 ml) soy sauce
2 tablespoons (2 × 15 ml) brown sugar
2 teaspoons (2 × 5 ml) white wine vinegar or lemon juice
2 cloves of garlic, crushed
4 tablespoons (4 × 15 ml) crunchy peanut butter
1 tablespoon (1 × 15 ml) olive or salad oil
1 tablespoon (1 × 15 ml) soy sauce
1 tablespoon (1 × 15 ml) lemon juice
$\frac{1}{2}$–1 teaspoon (2.5–5 ml) chilli powder
2 oz (50 g) creamed coconut
2 oz (50 g) grated onion
$\frac{1}{4}$ pint (150 ml) hot water
1 clove of garlic, crushed

Cut the chicken into bite-sized cubes and prick well with a fork. Mix together the soy sauce, one tablespoon (1 × 15 ml) of brown sugar, vinegar or lemon juice and garlic. Add the chicken cubes, toss, cover and leave for 1–2 hours to marinade.

Mix the creamed coconut with the hot water and beat well when the coconut has softened.

Fry the onion in oil until soft but not coloured, then fry the chilli powder for a moment. Add the peanut butter, the remaining tablespoon of brown sugar and then the creamed coconut. Blend well and cook gently until the sauce is fairly thick, stirring continuously. Then put it to one side.

Drain the chicken pieces and thread them onto skewers. Barbecue over hot coals for about 7–10 minutes, turning once and basting with the marinade. While the chicken is cooking, re-heat the sauce, adding the soy sauce, lemon juice and crushed garlic. When the chicken is cooked, lay the skewers on a bed of boiled rice which has been cooked in the kitchen, and spoon the peanut sauce over them.

Note : Pork and veal can be substituted in this recipe. Try alternating the meat on the skewers with chunks of pineapple which have been dipped in melted butter.

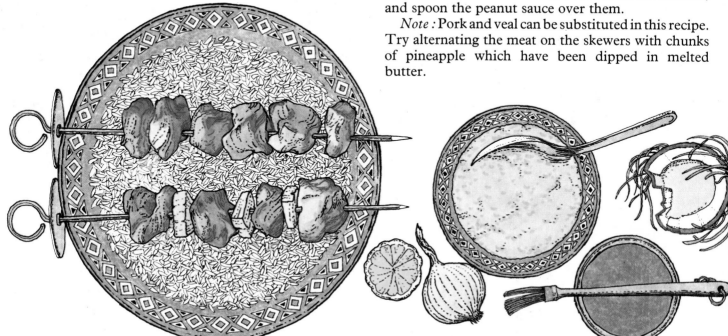

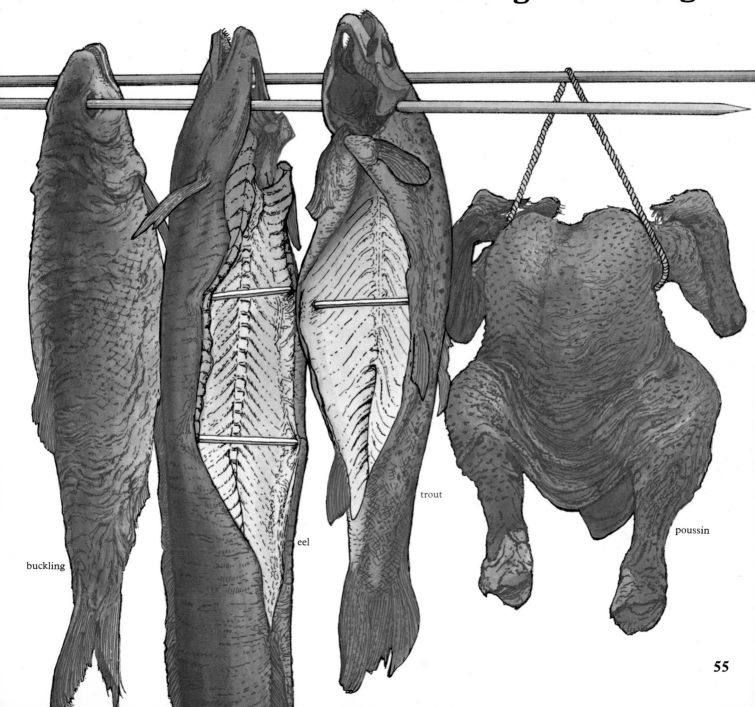

buckling

eel

trout

poussin

In a smoke-oven, food is either smoke-cooked or smoke-cured although sometimes a combination of both techniques is used. Unlike barbecuing on a closed fire, where the distance from fire to food is measured in inches, the distance in a smoke-oven from fire to food may be three feet or more. This results in lower cooking temperatures and therefore longer cooking times being needed, but the gentler heat environment prevents the meat from becoming case-hardened or even baked on the surface. The other speciality of a smoke-oven is, of course, that its smoky wood fire imparts delicious flavours to the taste of the food.

Oak, beech, elm, sycamore, hickory or the wood from most fruit trees can all contribute their special aromas. They are burnt in the form of sawdust, chips, twigs or sawn and split logs. Different cooking methods require varying burning and heating methods which may range from a powerful log fire to the gentle smouldering of a bowlful of sawdust. Sawdust needs little attention while it burns and once it is lit it will continue to smoulder for many hours. It is placed on a little tray made of foil, ignited with a glowing piece of charcoal, more charcoal and sawdust being added now and then to keep the fire going.

Buy wood and sawdust from a reliable source thereby making sure that no fuel from coniferous trees, such as pine, burns in your smoke-oven because these resinous woods give food an unpleasant flavour. Large sawmills do sometimes separate sawdust for special uses and another source for hardwoods may be an undertaker's yard! But if you live in the suburbs or near open land, look out for pruning activities in the late autumn. Another aspect of smoke-curing may well help to reduce the fuel problem: since food is usually smoked in batches there will at times be more than is needed for consumption at home. We, the authors, live in one of London's suburbs and quickly found that our friends and neighbours enjoyed the taste of our home-smoked produce and were only too glad to offer us wood in return.

The number of cooking methods possible with a smoke-oven is large, and after some time you will no doubt evolve your own combinations of the basic techniques. To begin with, however, it is worth trying out the three basic methods to see and experience the scope that is possible with this type of cooking. The three methods are: smoke-cooking (the shortest), hot-smoking, and cold-smoking (which takes the longest time).

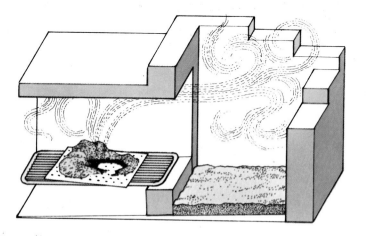

SMOKE-COOKING

This method is not only the fastest but also the simplest and is in fact very similar to smoke-cooking on barbecues with a closed fire or those with a foil-and-wire hood. Because of the fire to food distance, cooking times are roughly twice as long in the smoke-oven, and basting techniques differ too, since in the smoke-oven, pieces usually hang down from a single support instead of lying on a grill.

Whole, halved or pieces of chicken, turkey or duck are simply hung from long wire hooks or loops so that they can roast-cook in the hottest part of the chimney – nearest the fire. Fish is either suspended from hooks, or supported on a wire tray inside the chimney and turned carefully once.

To prevent meats and poultry from drying out, use freshly cut or damp wood and if none is available, immerse dry wood for 15 to 30 minutes (depending on diameter) beforehand in water. Water from the damp wood will be carried by the smoke to the meat, keeping it moist and juicy. Basting also counteracts evaporation that would dry out the food, spicing or flavouring it at the same time.

Start the fire two hours ahead of time so that when cooking begins it has become a bed of glowing coals that will ignite a fresh supply of wood quickly. This will also give the fire a chance to warm up the side walls of the chimney so that they begin to radiate heat.

If the fire seems to die down during cooking, open the vents, add kindling and a few pieces of charcoal but close the vents if the fire flares up and threatens to bake the food. Too hot a fire hardens the outer layer of the meat, preventing the inner parts from being fully cooked. It is essential to keep all cooking temperatures for fish below 180°F (82°C) and those for poultry under 240°F (115°C). A thermometer, scaled from 0° to 150°C is essential to check the actual heat in the oven and a bi-metallic model that has an outside dial will give readings without trouble at any time. Its sensitive stem protrudes through a narrow hole in the mortar to the inside of the chimney and additional holes can be provided to allow the temperatures for different cooking methods to be checked. It will be necessary to keep a moist cloth handy with which to wipe off now and then the film of creosote that builds up on the metal surface.

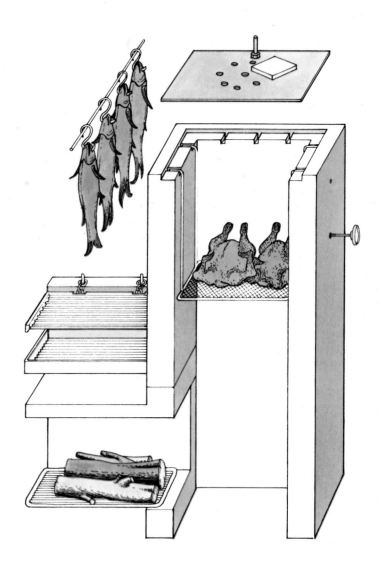

SMOKED SPARERIBS

Serves 4

1 rack of spareribs, weighing about $3\frac{1}{4}$ lb ($1\frac{1}{2}$ kg)
5 tablespoons (5 × 15 ml) salad oil
4 tablespoons (4 × 15 ml) soy sauce
4 tablespoons (4 × 15 ml) dry sherry
1 tablespoon (1 × 15 ml) brown sugar
1 small onion, chopped
A clove of garlic, crushed

Cut the rack of ribs into units of 4–5 ribs each and place them in a shallow dish. Combine all the ingredients, and pour over the meat. Cover and leave for an hour, turning occasionally. Use wire hooks to suspend the ribs in the chimney and cook at 190–220°F (88–93°C) for about three hours or until tender. Baste them hourly, tending the fire at the same time. Cut or snip ribs into serving pieces.

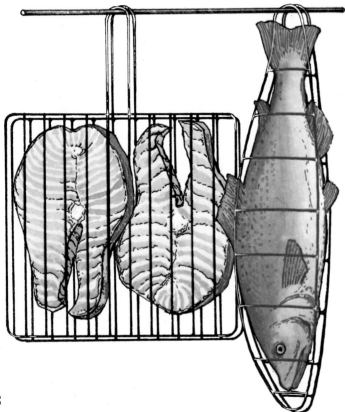

CHINESE SMOKED CHICKEN

Serves 8

Since smoked chickens can be stored in a freezer for up to one month, it is obviously more economical to cook more than one at a time. Measure out beforehand how many you will need to hang at the same level in the chimney with about 2 in (5 cm) between each bird and the same space between birds and walls. Temperatures in the chimney will be affected by outside winds and may be uneven so change the position of each rod or each bird at every basting.

2 × $2\frac{1}{2}$ lb ($1\frac{1}{4}$ kg) chickens
2 tablespoons (2 × 15 ml) soy sauce
4 tablespoons (4 × 15 ml) honey
$\frac{1}{2}$ teaspoon (2.5 ml) pepper
$\frac{1}{4}$ teaspoon (1.2 ml) garlic salt

Build up a fairly hot fire and when it is ready, mix the basting ingredients together in a jar and baste the chickens; then suspend them as illustrated. Close the chimney cover and adjust the vents so that the chickens cook at 200–225°F (93–107°C). Baste once every hour, adding new wood to the fire at the same time. Cook for 3–4 hours or until tender and check that no red or pink meat shows near the bones.

SMOKE-COOKED FISH

This is a simple method to give salmon or any white fish a delicate smoky flavour. Buy fish steaks or fish fillets and paint a thin film of olive or salad oil over the unskinned surfaces, then sprinkle with salt and pepper.

Pre-heat the chimney, then place the fish in a hinged wire basket and hang the basket in the chimney. Cook at 180°F (82°C) for two hours or until tender – test by flaking with a fork. When cold, serve with a crisp salad and buttered rye bread.

Here is a tip to save fuel and effort: if you only want to cook one or two portions, why not smoke-cook it at the same time as you are hot-smoking another batch of fish.

HOT AND COLD SMOKING

In the past, smoke-curing was widely used as a preservative to improve the keeping quality of fish and meat. The tarry creosote from the smouldering wood fire is deposited on the food and it is the antiseptic nature of this creosote that inhibits the development of bacteria which would otherwise spoil the food. In addition, hot smoke and heat from the fire dry out the tissues, thus increasing the keeping quality still further. That is why only dry woods are burnt in smoke-curing and a sunny day is preferred to a rainy one.

Nowadays, food is usually preserved by freezing during storage and transportation, while smoke-curing has come to be regarded as more of a means to improve or change the taste of staple foods.

In commercial installations, cold smoking is carried out at temperatures as low as 50–85°F (10–30°C); it is a lengthy process that needs many days or even weeks to complete and such work would take far too long for most amateurs. Fortunately, there is a way to drastically shorten the process by following a much reduced cold-smoking period by a short hot-smoking one as described on the following pages.

BRINING

Freshly caught fish will, of course, give the best results in any form of cooking but it is not always easy to buy especially in towns and suburbs. However frozen fish can be almost as good – as long as it is cured immediately after thawing. Poultry too is best cured when fresh although frozen birds can also be very tasty.

To improve both the keeping quality and the taste, foods to be smoke-cured must be immersed in a salt solution for a while. A simple way to do this is to immerse the food in a strong brine, made by dissolving 2 lb 6 oz of salt in 1 gallon of water (1.2 kg in $4\frac{1}{4}$ l). To dissolve the salt, part of the water is heated and poured hot over the crystals so that they rapidly dissolve before the remaining cold water is added.

During brining, the fish or meat must be totally immersed in the liquid and turned at intervals. Use a weighted lid that floats on the surface for fish, or stones placed in the cavities of birds to keep them from rising.

Of course, fish and poultry must always be washed, brined and smoked separately so as not to taint one with the taste of another. After brining, all products, except trout and eel, should be drained before smoking begins. You can use discarded brine as a weed killer.

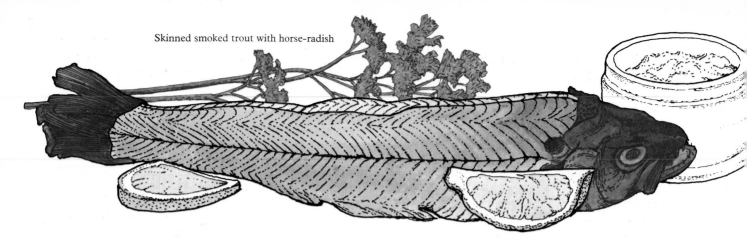

Skinned smoked trout with horse-radish

CHECKING AND TESTING

Because smoking processes can take a long time, it is always a good idea to keep a record of every batch that was smoked, noting the lengths of brining, draining and smoking times and the actual temperatures obtained. The best and only way to test food is to eat it, then overbrining or undersmoking can be detected and the timesheets corrected for the next batches. Such time sheets are particularly useful in case the fire should have gone out during a curing session and new times have to be worked out. It is no disaster when this happens during a cold-smoking period; try to estimate how long the fire was out by feeling the warmth of the oven walls, then light up again and compensate for the time lost plus the warming-up period needed to return to the correct temperature.

The smoking times given in the following recipes can only be approximate since moisture content and type of wood burnt, outside temperatures and humidity and also the manner of keeping a fire going, vary widely. Watch and develop your own routine of firemanship and stick to it to achieve consistency.

SMOKED TROUT

Buy enough trout, weighing not more than 8 oz to 1 lb (250–450 g) each, so that it fills your chimney comfortably with about $1\frac{1}{2}$ in (4 cm) between each fish. (As all fish become soft during cooking, heavier trout may part from the hook and fall down.) The trout should be gutted, its blood channel removed and the inside well washed under a running tap. The head is left on to take the hook for hanging up.

Immerse the fish in brine for one hour (see BRINING), and turn it occasionally. Then take it out and pierce a metal hook through the bony part just over the gills and near the vertebrae. Before hanging it in the chimney, insert a small piece of wood, a matchstick will do, to keep the belly flaps apart so that the smoke can reach a larger surface of the fish.

Cold-smoke the fish at roughly 80°F (26°C) for about seven hours until the skin feels dry. Then quickly heat up the oven with larger logs of wood to just under 180°F (82°C), keeping this hot-smoking temperature steady for about two hours. Do not exceed this temperature because the fish is now very flabby and may fall apart.

After hot-smoking, gently take the fish out and leave it to cool at room temperature. Allow it to mature for at least one day before eating. Surplus trout can always be stored in a deep freezer for a maximum of one month.

SMOKED EEL

Tasting nothing like 'jellied eel', this delicacy is much loved in Holland and Denmark where many smoking kilns still operate. Buy fresh eel with a diameter of at least $1\frac{1}{4}$ in (3.5 cm). The eel must be scrubbed to remove slime, then gutted and an incision made $1\frac{1}{2}$ in (4 cm) below the vent to remove the kidney. The head is left on.

Immerse the eel in brine for 15–25 minutes and then hook it from front to back for hanging up. Keep the body cavity open by inserting a few cocktail sticks along the opening.

Eels need no draining so they are hung straight in the smoke-oven and cold-smoked for about two hours at 90°F (32°C) after which the temperature is raised to 120°F (50°C) for half an hour. A final smoking period of one hour at 170°F (76°C) completes the curing process; larger and thicker eels need longer smoking at this final stage.

You can eat smoked eel after two days or store it in a refrigerator for up to five days. Freeze any remaining eel for up to three weeks.

BUCKLING

Starting off as an ordinary herring, buckling is well known and liked by the people who live along the coastlines of the North Sea. Although originally only herrings from the Baltic were used for this process, any healthy fresh or frozen herring can be cured to become a buckling.

The fish is brined whole with guts and milt intact for about three hours, then rinsed under cold running water before being hooked through the eyes. It is then hung up to drain for about three hours, depending on size.

Transferred to the smoke-oven, it is cold-smoked for half an hour at 85°F (30°C) after which the temperature is increased to hot-smoking at 160°F (71°C) and maintained for an hour. At the end of this hour, the fire should be made particularly smoky (by sprinkling damp sawdust or damp wood chips over

it) and the fish finally hot-smoked for another $1\frac{1}{2}$ hours at a constant 140°F (60°C). It will taste delicious the next day and any surplus buckling can be stored (with guts removed) in a deep freezer for up to three weeks.

SPRATS

Sprats also belong to the herring family. They are caught when about 5 in (12 cm) long and are brined and cured whole, just like buckling. Being small, they are best cooked on a wire tray in the smoke oven and turned over occasionally. Having little meat, they need far shorter brining and smoking times:

Brining for $\frac{1}{2}$ hour
Draining for one hour
Cold-smoking for 1 hour at 85°F (30°C)
Hot smoking for $\frac{1}{2}$ hour at 150°F (65°C)

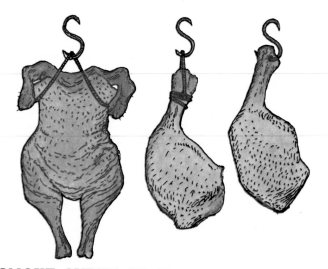

SMOKED DUCK AND GOOSE

These birds are better smoked when you have become familiar with your cooking techniques. Duck and geese contain a large amount of fat and need therefore longer (but not hotter) cooking times. Also, the fat ignites easily and flames may eventually reach the bird itself. To counteract this possibility wet the bed of sand at the chimney base and check the fire more often, keeping a water-spray handy in case of flare-ups. The high fat content may also lead to a rancid taste of the meat. To avoid this happening, maintain the temperature of the cold-smoking period as accurately as you can and without interruptions.

Buy birds weighing about 4–4½ lb (2 kg)
Deeply prick and brine for 2½–3½ hours
Drain and dry for one day
Carefully cold-smoke for 36 hours at 75°F (24°C)
Hot-smoke for 3–5 hours depending on size, at 200–240°F (93–115°C).

SMOKE-CURED CHICKEN

Choose birds weighing about 4 lb (1.8 kg) each and deeply prick with a fork all over the fleshy parts. This will help the brine to penetrate the flesh. Immerse in brine for 2½ hours, turning them occasionally.

After brining, string each bird as shown and hang them up to drain for one day.

Cold-smoking should take a long time to impart the smoky flavour gradually, so cold-smoke the chickens for two to three days depending on size at a temperature of about 70°F (24°C). This is a long time, but if you check your fire twice a day and leave an extra portion of sawdust on a foil pan between the embers late at night, the fire will continue to smoulder until morning. Remember the procedure mentioned earlier, should the fire go out.

Complete the process with a hot-smoking period at 220°–240°F (105°–118°C) for about two hours depending on size. If this process takes too long, use pieces or halved birds as these need less cooking time.

SMOKED TURKEY

Use the same process as for chicken, but you may have to increase the hot-smoking period until the turkey becomes tender.

Salads

Crunchy salads cleanse the palate and are refreshing with spicy barbecues. Every one knows lettuce salad, so ring the changes with one of the following suggestions.

BEAN SALAD
Serves 4

12 oz (300 g) cooked, tinned, fresh or frozen beans
1 clove of garlic
6 tablespoons (6 × 15 ml) French dressing

Cut the garlic clove in half and rub it round the inside of a bowl. Drain the beans well and place in the bowl with the French dressing. Toss well and if liked shake a little paprika over the top. Serve immediately.

COLE SLAW
Serves 4–5

1 small head of white cabbage
2 carrots, peeled and grated
1 eating apple, chopped
2 oz (50 g) raisins or sultanas
4 tablespoons (4 × 15 ml) French dressing
3 tablespoons (3 × 15 ml) mayonnaise

Finely slice or shred the cabbage, grate the carrots and chop the apple. Mix them together, cover and chill. Beat the French dressing and mayonnaise together until smooth. Just before serving, add the raisins or sultanas and cabbage mixture to the dressing and toss well.

CUCUMBER SALAD
Serves 3–4

1 large cucumber
1 tablespoon (1 × 15 ml) finely chopped parsley
Salt and freshly ground black pepper
French dressing

Peel and slice the cucumber finely. Place in a bowl and mix well with salt. Place a plate on top and weight it. Allow to stand for a few hours, then drain. Do this a few times. Just before serving remove the weight and plate, and toss the cucumber in a little French dressing and sprinkle with freshly ground black pepper and the parsley.

CURRIED POTATO SALAD
Serves 2–3

1 lb (450 g) waxy potatoes, peeled
4 tablespoons (4 × 15 ml) mayonnaise
1 tablespoon (1 × 15 ml) chopped parsley
1 teaspoon (1 × 5 ml) curry powder
1 carton sour cream

In a bowl mix together the mayonnaise, sour cream and curry powder, cover and chill in the refrigerator for at least one hour. Boil the peeled potatoes until just tender. Drain and dice. While still warm, add to the bowl of dressing and toss well. Sprinkle the parsley over the top and serve.

POTATO SALAD
Serves 2–3

1 lb (450 g) waxy potatoes, peeled
¼ pint (150 ml) mayonnaise, or French dressing
1–2 tablespoons (1–2 × 15 ml) finely chopped
  onion or chives
1 tablespoon (1 × 15 ml) chopped parsley
Salt and freshly ground white pepper

Boil the potatoes until just tender, then drain and dice them. While still warm, place in a bowl and add the mayonnaise or French dressing. Season lightly, add the onion or chives and mix gently with a spoon. Sprinkle the chopped parsley over the top just before serving.

Another tasty idea is to grill 2–3 rashers of bacon until crisp. Crush and sprinkle over the top of the potatoes.

SIMPLE SALAD
Serves 4

1 head of lettuce
French dressing
1 clove of garlic
½ a green pepper and ½ a red pepper
or 1 teaspoon (1 × 5 ml) chopped chives, chervil,
  tarragon or mixed herbs

Cut the clove of garlic in half and rub round the inside of a bowl. Wash the lettuce leaves and pat dry, then tear them into bite-sized pieces. Either add the finely sliced red and green peppers to the lettuce and toss in the French dressing, or add any of the above herbs to the dressing before pouring it over the lettuce. Toss well.

SPINACH SALAD
Serves 4

1 lettuce heart
4 oz (100 g) fresh spinach
4 tablespoons (4 × 15 ml) olive oil
2 tablespoons (2 × 15 ml) white wine vinegar
2 teaspoons (2 × 5 ml) grated lemon rind
½ teaspoon (2.5 ml) dried basil
or 1½ teaspoons (1½ × 5 ml) fresh basil
6 spring onions, chopped

In a jug mix together the oil, vinegar, lemon rind and basil. Leave to stand for an hour or two. Wash the spinach well, cut out and discard the stalks, then pat dry or shake really well. Wash the lettuce leaves and pat dry. Tear the spinach and lettuce into small pieces and pile into a bowl. Add the chopped onions to the bowl and then pour over the dressing. Toss well and serve immediately.

TOMATO SALAD
Serves 4

1 lb (450 g) firm tomatoes
1 medium sized onion, thinly sliced
1 tablespoon (1 × 15 ml) French dressing
Salt and freshly ground black pepper
Chopped parsley or chives for garnish

Cut the tomatoes into thin slices and arrange in the bottom of a dish, season and sprinkle a few onion rings over them. Continue in layers until all the tomatoes and onion are used up. Pour the French dressing over the top and leave for an hour. Just before serving, sprinkle the parsley or chives over the top.

Breads, butters, sauces and marinades

GARLIC BREAD, ONION BREAD, HERB BREAD or ANCHOVY BREAD
Serves 6–8

1 French stick
Garlic, onion, herb or anchovy butter

Cut the bread at 1 in (2.5 cm) intervals cutting to, but not through the crust. Spread the garlic, onion, herb or anchovy butter between the slices of bread. Wrap the loaf in a sheet of greased foil (dull side on the outside), seeing that the edges are well sealed. Place the parcel on the grill over medium heat and cook for about 15 minutes, turning once. Before serving, cut through the bottom crust to free the slices.

FLAVOURED BUTTERS

Flavoured (or seasoned) butters add variety to plain grills and are a good standby for the cook who is in a hurry. They can be used with meat, poultry, fish, breads and vegetables. Shape them into logs and wrap them in waxed paper or aluminium foil, then refrigerate. It is not advisable to keep the butters more than a week as their flavours will gradually deteriorate. When melted they can be used as a baste.

ANCHOVY BUTTER
For hamburgers, beef steaks, fish and bread
Drain a can of anchovies and either pound or finely chop the fillets. Cream 4 oz (100 g) butter or margarine with $\frac{1}{2}$ teaspoon (2.5 ml) lemon juice, 1 clove of garlic finely minced (optional) and a pinch of paprika, then gradually add the anchovies.

CURRY BUTTER
For pork or lamb chops and poultry
Cream 4 oz (100 g) butter or margarine with 2–4 teaspoons (2–4 × 5 ml) curry powder, 2 teaspoons (2 × 5 ml) lemon juice and a shake of tabasco sauce.

GARLIC BUTTER
For hamburgers, beef steaks, lamb chops, fish, bread and baked potatoes
Cream 4 oz (100 g) butter or margarine with 1 teaspoon (1 × 5 ml) minced garlic and 2 tablespoons (2 × 15 ml) chopped parsley.

HERB BUTTER

For hamburgers, beef steaks, lamb chops, poultry, fish, bread and baked potatoes

Cream 4 oz (100 g) butter or margarine with 1 teaspoon (1 × 5 ml) crushed dried rosemary, tarragon or marjoram, 2 teaspoons (2 × 5 ml) chopped parsley, ¼ teaspoon (1.2 ml) salt and a dash of freshly ground pepper.

MAÎTRE D'HÔTEL BUTTER

For grills and as a baste for poultry and fish

Cream 4 oz (100 g) butter or margarine with 2 teaspoons (2 × 5 ml) lemon juice, 1 tablespoon (1 × 15 ml) chopped parsley, ¼ teaspoon (1.2 ml) salt, dash of freshly ground black pepper or cayenne and a pinch of thyme (optional).

MINT BUTTER

For lamb, poultry and baked potatoes

Cream 4 oz (100 g) butter or margarine with 1 tablespoon (1 × 15 ml) chopped mint leaves, ¼ teaspoon (1.2 ml) salt and a dash of freshly ground pepper.

MUSTARD BUTTER

For hamburgers, beef steaks, frankfurters and fish

Cream 4 oz (100 g) butter or margarine with 2-4 teaspoons (2-4 × 5 ml) continental mustard, 2 teaspoons (2 × 5 ml) lemon juice, ¼ teaspoon (1.2 ml) salt and a dash of freshly ground pepper.

ONION BUTTER

For hamburgers, beef steaks, bread and baked potatoes

Cream 4 oz (100 g) butter or margarine with 1 teaspoon (1 × 5 ml) Worcestershire sauce, ½ teaspoon (2.5 ml) lemon juice, ¼ teaspoon (1.2 ml) freshly ground pepper, ¼ teaspoon (1.2 ml) dry mustard. Beat well then fold in 2 tablespoons (2 × 15 ml) chopped parsley and 1-2 tablespoons (1-2 × 15 ml) grated onion or 1 tablespoon (1 × 15 ml) chopped chives.

SWEET & SOUR SAUCE

For pork, spareribs, poultry and fish steaks

½ pint (300 ml) crushed pineapple pulp
¼ pint (150 ml) dry white wine
2 tablespoons (2 × 15 ml) white wine vinegar
2 tablespoons (2 × 15 ml) olive or salad oil
2 tablespoons (2 × 15 ml) brown sugar
1 tablespoon (1 × 15 ml) soy sauce
2 teaspoons (2 × 5 ml) onion, finely chopped
1 teaspoon (1 × 5 ml) lemon juice
1 teaspoon (1 × 5 ml) paprika
½ teaspoon (2.5 ml) garlic salt
optional:
1 tablespoon (1 × 15 ml) green pepper, chopped or
1 tablespoon (1 × 15 ml) pimento chopped

Combine all the ingredients in a saucepan and simmer for 10-15 minutes, stirring from time to time.

HONEY AND ROSEMARY SAUCE

For lamb chops, pork chops and ham

6 tablespoons (6 × 15 ml) honey
6 tablespoons (6 × 15 ml) prepared mustard
1 teaspoon (1 × 5 ml) salt
½ teaspoon (2.5 ml) rosemary
¼ teaspoon (1.2 ml) freshly ground pepper

Mix together all the ingredients and baste lamb, pork chops or ham during the last half of cooking time.

EASY BEEF SAUCE
For beef steaks and hamburgers

1 tablespoon (1 × 15 ml) ketchup
1 tablespoon (1 × 15 ml) Worcestershire sauce
1 tablespoon (1 × 15 ml) vinegar
1 tablespoon (1 × 15 ml) brown sugar or clear honey
1 dessertspoon (1 × 10 ml) butter or margarine, melted
½ teaspoon (2.5 ml) ready prepared mustard
Dash of lemon juice

Mix all the ingredients together, brush on both sides of steaks or hamburgers and leave to stand for half an hour. Brush the meat again with the sauce while barbecuing.

EASY CHICKEN SAUCE
For chicken or turkey

6 tablespoons (6 × 15 ml) dry white wine
6 tablespoons (6 × 15 ml) olive or salad oil
1 teaspoon (1 × 5 ml) onion salt
2 cloves of garlic, minced

Combine all the ingredients in a small saucepan and heat until boiling, then remove from heat. Use as a basting sauce during the last half of the cooking period.

CURRY MARINADE
For lamb, spareribs and chicken

8 fl oz (200 ml) tomato ketchup
4 fl oz (100 ml) boiling water
1 tablespoon (1 × 15 ml) lemon juice
1½ teaspoons (1½ × 5 ml) curry powder
1 teaspoon (1 × 5 ml) freshly ground black pepper
1 chicken stock cube

Dissolve the cube in the boiling water. Add the remaining ingredients and stir well. Marinade the food for 3-4 hours, reserving the remaining marinade for basting during the last half of the cooking period.

FISH MARINADE

6 fl oz (150 ml) rosé wine or apple juice
4 tablespoons (4 × 15 ml) lemon juice
2 tablespoons (2 × 15 ml) freshly chopped onion
½ teaspoon (2.5 ml) monosodium glutamate (optional)
A few drops of angostura bitters

Combine all the ingredients and marinade the fish or fillets for 2 hours.

RED MEAT MARINADE

4 fl oz (100 ml) olive or salad oil
4 fl oz (100 ml) dry red wine
4 fl oz (100 ml) red wine vinegar
1 small carrot, grated
1 small onion, grated
2 cloves of garlic, minced
4 cloves
1 bay leaf
3 sprigs of fresh parsley
2 sprigs of fresh thyme
Salt and freshly ground black pepper

Mix together the oil, wine and vinegar and then add the remaining ingredients. Pour over the food, cover and leave to marinade for a few hours, turning occasionally.

GARLIC MARINADE
For pork, beef, chicken

4 tablespoons (4 × 15 ml) soy sauce
4 tablespoons (4 × 15 ml) olive or salad oil
2 tablespoons (2 × 15 ml) tomato ketchup
1 tablespoon (1 × 15 ml) vinegar
¼ teaspoon (1.2 ml) freshly ground black pepper
2 cloves of garlic, crushed

Mix together all the ingredients and pour over the food. Leave to marinade for a few hours.

ARMENIAN HERB MARINADE
For lamb or chicken

6 tablespoons (6 × 15 ml) olive or salad oil
6 tablespoons (6 × 15 ml) grated onion
4 tablespoons (4 × 15 ml) lemon juice
4 tablespoons (4 × 15 ml) chopped parsley
1 teaspoon (1 × 5 ml) salt
1 teaspoon (1 × 5 ml) marjoram or rosemary
1 teaspoon (1 × 5 ml) thyme
1 teaspoon (1 × 5 ml) fenugreek (optional)

Combine all the ingredients before pouring over the food. Cover and leave to marinade for 2 hours, turning occasionally.

EASY BARBECUE MARINADE
For meat, poultry or fish. It can also be used as a basting sauce.

3 tablespoons (3 × 15 ml) olive or salad oil
3 tablespoons (3 × 15 ml) dry sherry
2 tablespoons (2 × 15 ml) Worcestershire sauce or
   soy sauce
1 teaspoon (1 × 5 ml) prepared mustard
1-2 cloves of garlic, minced
Dash of freshly ground black pepper

Combine all the ingredients and pour over the food. Cover and refrigerate, turning occasionally.
Marinade salmon and chicken for 2 hours, steaks for 3-4 hours, roasts for 24-48 hours.

POULTRY MARINADE

8 fl oz (200 ml) dry white wine
4 fl oz (100 ml) white wine vinegar
2 medium onions, sliced
2 sprigs of marjoram, tarragon or rosemary
Salt and freshly ground black pepper

Mix the wine and vinegar together, then add the remaining ingredients. Pour over the food, cover and leave to marinade for a few hours, turning occasionally.

HERB MARINADE
For lamb or poultry

3 tablespoons (3 × 15 ml) red or white wine vinegar
3 tablespoons (3 × 15 ml) olive or salad oil
1 tablespoon (1 × 15 ml) lemon juice
2 teaspoons (2 × 5 ml) crushed rosemary, tarragon
   or mixed herbs
1 teaspoon (1 × 5 ml) salt
½ teaspoon (2.5 ml) freshly ground black pepper
1 or 2 cloves of garlic

Combine all the ingredients in a saucepan and heat until simmering. Cover, remove from heat and allow to stand for an hour before pouring over lamb or poultry. Marinade for 2-4 hours.

TERIYAKI MARINADE
For beef, spareribs, poultry and fish. It can also be used as a basting sauce.

4 tablespoons (4 × 15 ml) soy sauce
2 tablespoons (2 × 15 ml) olive or salad oil
2 tablespoons (2 × 15 ml) clear honey or brown sugar
1 tablespoon (1 × 15 ml) red wine vinegar or dry
   red wine
1 teaspoon (1 × 5 ml) freshly grated root ginger
or a good pinch of ground ginger
1 teaspoon (1 × 5 ml) monosodium glutamate
1-2 cloves of garlic, crushed

Combine all the ingredients and pour over the food. Cover and refrigerate, turning occasionally.
Marinade fish for 2-4 hours, spareribs or chicken for 4-8 hours, beef for 6-8 hours.

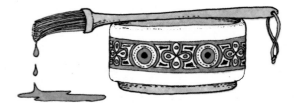

Desserts

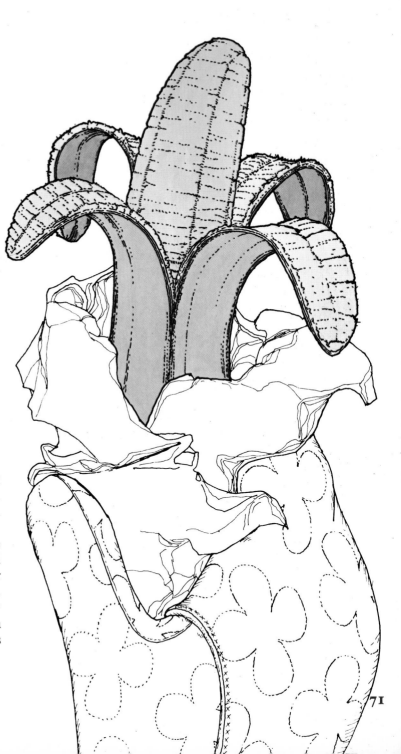

If, after barbecuing a succulent main course, the cook has any strength left and his guests still clamour for more, here are a few simple ideas for using the last dying embers of charcoal.

FOIL WRAPPED BANANAS
Serves 4

4 large yellow bananas with green tips
4 fl oz (100 ml) maple syrup or rum
2 tablespoons (2 × 15 ml) lemon juice
Pinch of salt
Pinch of brown sugar

Peel the bananas but save the skins. In a bowl, mix together the maple syrup or rum, lemon juice, salt and brown sugar. Place the bananas in the mixture and leave to marinade for about 30 minutes, turning once. Put the bananas back in their skins, keeping the marinade to serve later. Wrap each banana in greased foil seeing that the edges are well sealed. Barbecue over medium heat for about 15 minutes, turning once. Unwrap the packages, remove the bananas from their skins and serve them with scoops of vanilla ice cream or pass round a bowl of thickly whipped cream. Pass round any remaining marinade.

SKEWERED BANANAS

Serves 4

4 large firm bananas
4 oranges
2 tablespoons (2 × 15 ml) lemon juice
1 tablespoon (1 × 15 ml) brown sugar
¼ teaspoon (1.2 ml) cinnamon

Leave the skin on the bananas and cut them into diagonal slices about 1 in (2.5 cm) thick. Leave the peel on the oranges and cut them into thick wedges. Mix together the brown sugar and cinnamon. Dip the cut banana ends into the lemon juice and then dunk in the brown sugar mixture. Thread the pieces onto the skewers, piercing them through the skin, alternating with the orange wedges, again piercing through the skin. Barbecue over medium heat, turning occasionally until the fruit is hot through and the banana peel turns brown.

BARBECUED APPLE RINGS

Serves 4

4-6 medium cooking apples
4 tablespoons (4 × 15 ml) brown sugar
1 teaspoon (1 × 5 ml) ground cinnamon
2 oz (50 g) butter

Wash and core the apples, but do not peel them, then cut them into 1 in (2.5 cm) thick slices. Mix together the sugar and cinnamon. Brush both sides of each apple slice with melted butter and barbecue them over medium heat for 8 minutes. Turn and sprinkle the surfaces with the sugar mixture and continue to cook for a further 8-10 minutes or until tender. Serve with a bowl of thickly whipped cream.

SKEWERED MARSHMALLOWS

Serves 4

32 Marshmallows
10 fl oz (283 g) bottled chocolate sauce
1 family block (483 ml) vanilla ice cream

Thread about 8 marshmallows on each skewer. Pour the chocolate sauce into a pan and place to one side of the grill to heat through very gently. Toast the marshmallows over hot coals until they are soft inside and brown on the outside. When they are ready, push them off the skewers into the chocolate sauce, stir once or twice and then spoon them over scoops of vanilla ice cream.

FOIL BAKED APPLES

Serves 4

4 large cooking apples
4 tablespoons (4 × 15 ml) brown sugar
4 tablespoons (4 × 15 ml) seedless raisins
Butter

Wash and core the apples, but do not peel them. Score a line round the middle of each one. Place each apple in the middle of an 8 in (20 cm) square piece of greased foil. Put a knob of butter in each cavity, then a tablespoon of sugar mixed with a tablespoon of raisins. Finally top with another knob of butter. Wrap the foil securely over the top of each apple and barbecue either over medium heat for about 45 minutes, turning once, or directly on low/medium coals for about 30 minutes. Serve with a bowl of whipped cream.

Note : For baked spiced apples, replace the sugar and seedless raisins with 8 tablespoons (8 × 15 ml) granulated sugar and 1 teaspoon (1 × 5 ml) ground cinnamon. Prepare and cook as above.

Children's parties

Children love to join in barbecuing, since the sizzling food, the aroma of cooking and the glow of an open fire hold a great fascination for any youngster.

Of course, it is only common sense that the younger the child, the more vital is the presence of an adult. If a child of, say, 10 years is to help with the cooking, it will need to be equipped as you would be yourself – with thick mittens, an apron and a basic knowledge of how to deal with emergencies.

The recipes that follow are easily prepared, simple to cook, and contribute much enjoyment to any children's party. For kebab barbecuing, place the ingredients in separate bowls and allow the children to make up their own combinations.

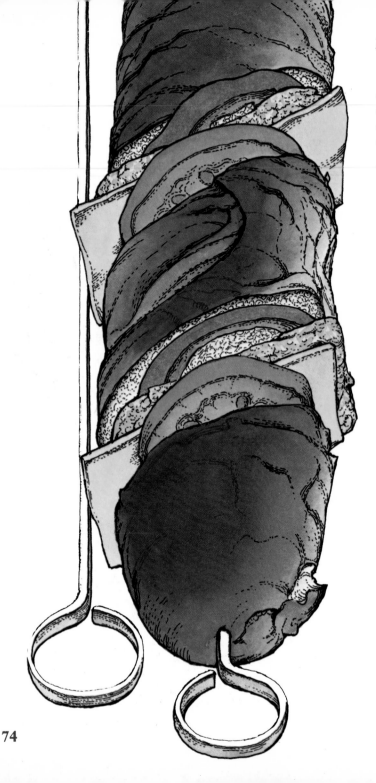

MEAT, CHEESE AND VEGETABLE LOAF
Serves 7–10

1 loaf of French bread
Thin slices of corned beef
Thin slices of Cheddar or processed cheese
Thin slices of tomato
Thin slices of green pepper
4–5 oz (100–125 g) butter or margarine
1–2 cloves of garlic, minced
1 tablespoon (1 × 15 ml) chopped parsley
Dash of salt and freshly ground black pepper

Cream together the butter or margarine, garlic and parsley and season lightly. Cut the loaf diagonally, not wholly through, into 1½ in (4 cm) slices. Spread the butter on both sides of the slices. Place a tomato slice, cheese slice, corned beef slice and a green pepper ring in each cut. Stick a skewer through the loaf lengthways and then wrap well with foil. Barbecue over medium heat, turning frequently, for about 20 minutes when the cheese should have melted. Remove the foil and skewer, cut through the remaining crust before serving the chunks on plates.

HAM AND CHEESE ROLLS
Serves 4

4 thin slices cooked ham
4 thin slices Cheddar or processed cheese
3 oz (75 g) butter or margarine
2–3 teaspoons (2–3 × 5 ml) horseradish sauce or
  mild mustard
2 tablespoons grated onion
4 soft rolls

Mix together the butter, horseradish sauce (or mustard) and onion, cream well. Split the rolls and spread the mixture over cut surfaces. Place a folded slice of ham and a slice of cheese between the halves. Wrap each roll in greased aluminium foil and barbecue over medium heat for about 15 minutes, turning frequently.

SURPRISE BURGERS
Serves 6

2 lb (1 kg) finely minced beef
1 lb (450 g) grated Cheddar cheese
2 teaspoons (2 × 5 ml) Worcestershire sauce
2 teaspoons (2 × 5 ml) ready mixed mustard
1 teaspoon (1 × 5 ml) salt
½ teaspoon (2.5 ml) freshly ground black pepper
1 medium onion finely grated
2 oz (50 g) butter, melted
6 soft rolls

Mix together the beef, Worcestershire sauce, mustard, salt, pepper and onion. Divide into 12 portions and shape into thin patties. Heap the grated cheese in the middle of six of the patties, top each with another patty and press the edges together well to seal. Barbecue over hot coals for about 6 minutes (medium), baste with the melted butter and turn only once. Split and toast the rolls during the last few minutes of cooking, on the grill, sandwich the burgers and serve immediately.

CHEESEY HOT DOGS
Serves 4

4 frankfurters
4 long rolls
4 strips of Cheddar cheese
Butter or margarine
4–8 rashers of streaky bacon

Cut open each frankfurter lengthways and place a strip of Cheddar cheese between the halves. Wrap a rasher or two of bacon round each frankfurter securing with wooden cocktail sticks. Make 4 foil pans large enough to take a frankfurter in each, and making sure that the wooden sticks do not tear the foil. Barbecue over medium heat until the bacon is crisp and the cheese has melted. Remove the wooden sticks and serve in toasted buttered rolls.

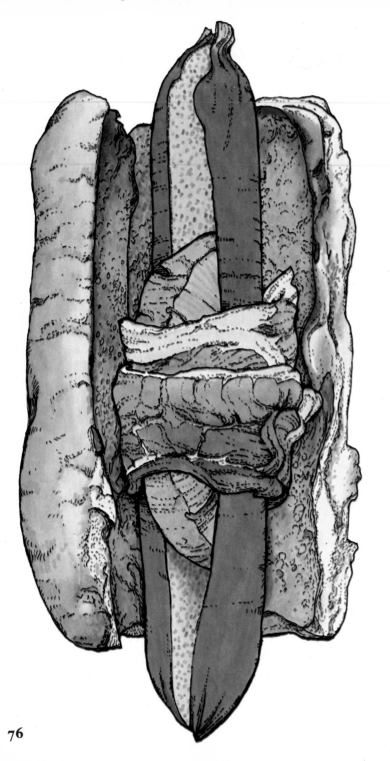

HOT DOGS
Serves 4

4 frankfurters
4 long rolls
Butter or margarine
Mustard or ketchup

Barbecue the frankfurters over medium heat for about 8 minutes, turning frequently. Just before they are cooked, split and toast the rolls and then butter them. Serve with the frankfurters in the rolls and garnish either with mustard or ketchup.

NUTTY HOT DOGS
Serves 4

4 frankfurters
4 long rolls
Crunchy peanut butter

Barbecue the frankfurters over medium heat for about 8 minutes, turning frequently. Just before they are cooked, split and toast the rolls and then spread the cut surfaces lavishly with the peanut butter. Serve with the frankfurters sandwiched between the rolls.

PINEAPPLE HOT DOGS
Serves 8

8 frankfurters
8 long rolls
Butter or margarine
8–16 rashers of streaky bacon
$1 \times 8\frac{1}{4}$ oz can (234 g) sliced pineapple rings

Cut open each frankfurter lengthways and place half a slice of a pineapple ring between the two halves. Wrap a rasher or two of bacon round each frankfurter securing with wooden cocktail sticks. Barbecue over medium heat until the bacon is crisp all round. Remove the wooden sticks before serving in toasted, buttered rolls.

Children's party drinks

Cooling drinks compliment hot barbecued food perfectly, even on an overcast day. Have the glasses and ingredients ready in the kitchen so that the drinks can be quickly mixed and served immediately with the food.

MILK SHAKES
Serves 4

1½ pints (900 ml) chilled milk
4 tablespoons (4 × 15 ml) vanilla ice cream
4 tablespoons (4 × 15 ml) heaped, of jam – eg cherry, peach, strawberry, raspberry, blackberry etc.

Put all the ingredients, about half at a time, into a blender and blend until fluffy. Pour into four glasses and serve immediately.

MINTED LIME REFRESHER
Serves 4

4 sprigs of mint, crushed
Concentrated lime cordial
Soda water
8 ice cubes

Put the crushed mint into four tall glasses. Cover with about ½ in (1 cm) of lime cordial then add two ice cubes per glass and top up with soda water. Serve immediately.

LIME AND GINGER FIZZ
Serves 6

1 packet of lime flavoured jelly
1 large bottle of ginger beer
Boiling water
12 mint leaves
A tray of ice cubes

Tear the jelly into cubes and place in a measuring jug. Add enough boiling water to make up to half a pint and stir until the jelly has dissolved. Pour into a bowl. Wash and pat dry the mint leaves. Add the ginger beer and ice cubes to the bowl and stir well. Pour into six glasses and float two mint leaves on top of each. Serve immediately.

MINT 'N CHOC
Serves 4-6

2 pints (1 litre) of milk
4 oz (100 g) milk chocolate
2 tablespoons (2 × 15 ml) thickly whipped cream
½ teaspoon (2.5 ml) peppermint essence
Mint leaves for decoration

Dissolve the chocolate in hot milk and then add the peppermint essence. When cool, pour into four or six glasses, top up with the cream and decorate with the mint leaves.

PARTY PUNCH
Serves 8

2 pints (1 litre) apple juice
12 fl oz (340 ml) ginger beer
4 tablespoons (4 × 15 ml) raspberry milk shake syrup
2 small red eating apples

Chill the apple juice and ginger beer in the refrigerator for 1–2 hours. Wash the apples, do not peel them, cut them into quarters and remove the core. Slice them finely. Pour the apple juice into a bowl, add the syrup and stir well. Add the ginger beer to the apple juice, stir well and float the apple slices on top. Serve immediately.

A good thirst quencher to accompany all barbecue main courses.

°C °F

150 — 300
140 — 290
— 280
130 — 270
— 260
120 — 250
— 240
110 — 230
— 220
100 — 210
— 200
90 — 190
— 180
80 — 170
— 160
70 — 150
60 — 140
— 130
50 — 120
— 110
40 — 100
30 — 90
— 80
20 — 70
— 60
10 — 50
— 40
0 — 32

Please note that the metric measures in this book are not exact conversions but have been rounded up.

Weights and Measures and their approximate equivalents

Liquid measures

BRITISH IMPERIAL	METRIC
1 gallon (4 quarts)	4.5 litres
1 quart (2 pints) = 40 fl oz	1.1 litre
1 pint (4 gills) = 20 fl oz	0.5 litre

METRIC	BRITISH IMPERIAL
1 litre (10 deci-litres)	35 fl oz (or 1.7 pints)
1 deci-litre (100 milli-litres)	3.5 fl oz

Dry or solid measures

BRITISH IMPERIAL	METRIC
1 lb (16 oz)	450 grams
1 oz	25 grams

METRIC	BRITISH IMPERIAL
1 kilogram (1000 grams)	2 lb 3 oz
100 grams	3.5 oz

Index – Recipes

The authors wish to thank Baker Perkins Ltd., for
their advice on chimney designs; Pat Simon MA MW
for many helpful hints on wine; Nicholas Kurth for
his engineering contribution to the grill-mechanisms
and Gordon Fielden for his help in preparing the MSS.